180 Days of PRACTICE

GRADE 3

HANDS-ON

STEAM

| Science | Technology | Engineering | Arts | Mathematics |

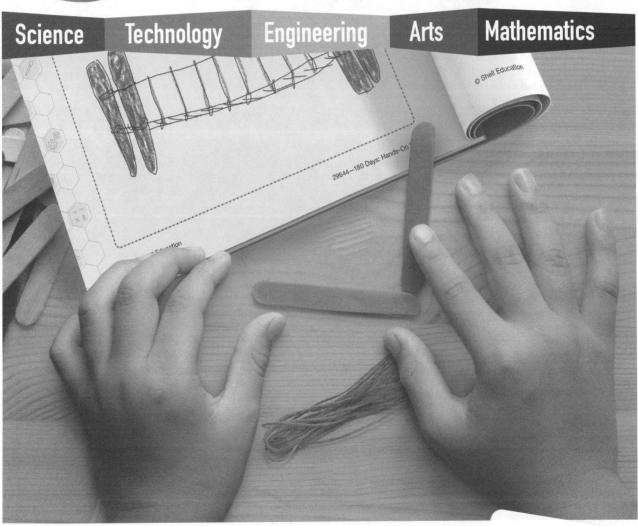

Kristin Kemp, M.A.Ed.

Program Credits

Corinne Burton, M.A.Ed., *Publisher*
Emily R. Smith, M.A.Ed., *VP of Content Development*
Véronique Bos, *Creative Director*
Lynette Ordoñez, *Content Manager*
Melissa Laughlin, *Editor*
Jill Malcolm, *Graphic Designer*
David Slayton, *Assistant Editor*

Image Credits

p.55 Jill Malcolm; all other images Shutterstock and/or iStock

Standards

NGSS Lead States. 2013. *Next Generation Science Standards: For States, By States.* Washington, DC: The National Academies Press.
© 2021 TESOL International Association
© 2021 Board of Regents of the University of Wisconsin System

A division of Teacher Created Materials
5482 Argosy Avenue
Huntington Beach, CA 92649
www.tcmpub.com/shell-education
ISBN 978-1-4258-2530-0
© 2022 Shell Educational Publishing, Inc.
Printed in USA. WOR004

Table of Contents

Research

The Importance of STEAM Education

STEAM education is a powerful approach to learning that continues to gain momentum and support across the globe. STEAM is the integration of science, technology, engineering, the arts, and mathematics to design solutions for real-world problems. Students must learn how to question, explore, and analyze natural phenomena. With these skills in hand, students understand the complexity of available information and are empowered to become independent learners and problem solvers.

The content and practices of STEAM education are strong components of a balanced instructional approach, ensuring students are college- and career-ready. The application of STEAM practices in the classroom affords teachers opportunities to challenge students to apply new knowledge. Students of all ages can design and build structures, improve existing products, and test innovative solutions to real-world problems. STEAM instruction can be as simple as using recycled materials to design a habitat for caterpillars discovered on the playground and as challenging as designing a solution to provide clean water to developing countries. The possibilities are endless.

Blending arts principles with STEM disciplines prepares students to be problem solvers, creative collaborators, and thoughtful risk-takers. Even students who do not choose a career in a STEAM field will benefit because these skills can be translated into almost any career. Students who become STEAM proficient are prepared to answer complex questions, investigate global issues, and develop solutions for real-world challenges. Rodger W. Bybee (2013, 64) summarizes what is expected of students as they join the workforce:

> As literate adults, individuals should be competent to understand STEM-related global issues; recognize scientific from other nonscientific explanations; make reasonable arguments based on evidence; and, very important, fulfill their civic duties at the local, national, and global levels.

Likewise, STEAM helps students understand how concepts are connected as they gain proficiency in the Four Cs: creativity, collaboration, critical thinking, and communication.

Research *(cont.)*

Defining STEAM

STEAM is an integrated way of preparing students for the twenty-first century world. It places an emphasis on understanding science and mathematics while learning engineering skills. By including art, STEAM recognizes that the creative aspect of any project is integral to good design—whether designing an experiment or an object.

Science

Any project or advancement builds on prior science knowledge. Science focuses on learning and applying specific content, cross-cutting concepts, and scientific practices that are relevant to the topic or project.

Technology

This is what results from the application of scientific knowledge and engineering. It is something that is created to solve a problem or meet a need. Some people also include the *use* of technology in this category. That is, tools used by scientists and engineers to solve problems. In addition to computers and robots, technology can include nets used by marine biologists, anemometers used by meteorologists, computer software used by mathematicians, and so on.

Engineering

This is the application of scientific knowledge to meet a need, solve a problem, or address phenomena. For example, engineers design bridges to withstand huge loads. Engineering is also used to understand phenomena, such as in designing a way to test a hypothesis. When problems arise, such as those due to earthquakes or rising sea levels, engineering is required to design solutions to the problems. On a smaller scale, a homeowner might want to find a solution to their basement flooding.

Art

In this context, art equals creativity and creative problem-solving. For example, someone might want to test a hypothesis but be stumped as to how to set up the experiment. Perhaps you have a valuable painting. You think there is another valuable image below the first layer of paint on the canvas. You do not want to destroy the painting on top. A creative solution is needed. Art can also include a creative or beautiful design that solves a problem. For example, the Golden Gate Bridge is considered both an engineering marvel and a work of art.

Mathematics

This is the application of mathematics to real-world problems. Often, this includes data analysis—such as collecting data, graphing it, analyzing the data, and then communicating that analysis. It may also include taking mathematical measurements in the pursuit of an answer. The idea is not to learn new math, but rather to apply it; however, some mathematics may need to be learned to solve the specific problem. Isaac Newton, for example, is famous for *inventing* calculus to help him solve problems in understanding gravity and motion.

Research *(cont.)*

The Engineering Design Process

The most essential component of STEAM education is the engineering design process. This process is an articulated approach to problem solving in which students are guided through the iterative process of solving problems and refining solutions to achieve the best possible outcomes. There are many different versions of the engineering design process, but they all have the same basic structure and goals. As explained in Appendix I of NGSS (2013), "At any stage, a problem-solver can redefine the problem or generate new solutions to replace an idea that just isn't working out."

Each unit in this resource presents students with a design challenge in an authentic and engaging context. The practice pages guide and support students through the engineering design process to solve problems or fulfill needs.

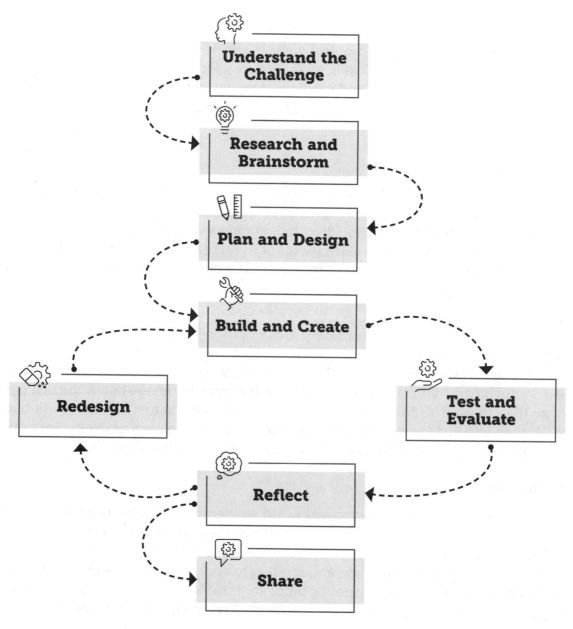

Research (cont.)

How to Facilitate Successful STEAM Challenges

There are some basic rules to remember as your students complete STEAM challenges.

Both independent and collaborative work should be included.

Astronaut and inventor Ellen Ochoa is well-known for working a robotic arm in space. About that experience she said, "It's fun to work the robotic arm, in part because it's a team effort." She recognized that she was getting credit for something amazing that happened because of the collaborative work of hundreds of people.

Students need time to think through a project, both on their own and together with others. It is often best to encourage students to start by thinking independently. One student may think of a totally different solution than another student. Once they come together, students can merge aspects of each other's ideas to devise something even better.

Failure is a step in the process.

During the process of trying to invent a useful light bulb, Thomas Edison famously said, "I have not failed. I've just found 10,000 ways that won't work." People are innovating when they are failing because it is a chance to try something new. The STEAM challenges in this book intentionally give students chances to improve their designs. Students should feel free to innovate as much as possible, especially the first time around. Then, they can build on what they learned and try again.

Some students get stuck thinking there is one right way. There are almost always multiple solutions to a problem. For example, attaching train cars together used to be very dangerous. In the late nineteenth century, different solutions to this problem were invented in England and the United States to make the process safer. Both solutions worked, and both were used! Encourage students to recognize that there are usually different ways to solve problems. Discuss the pros and cons of the various solutions that students generate.

Research *(cont.)*

How to Facilitate Successful STEAM Challenges *(cont.)*

Getting inspiration from others is an option.

Students worry a lot about copying. It is important to remind them that all breakthroughs come on the shoulders of others. No one is working in a vacuum, and it is okay to get inspiration and ideas from others. It is also important to give credit to the people whose work and ideas inspired others. Students may see this as cheating, but they should be encouraged to see that they had a great enough idea that others recognized it and wanted to build on it.

The struggle is real—and really important.

Most people do not like to fail. And it can be frustrating not to know what to do or what to try next. Lonnie Johnson, engineer and toy inventor, advises, "Persevere. That's what I always say to people. There's no easy route." Try to support students during this struggle, as amazing innovations can emerge from the process. Further, students feel great when they surprise themselves with success after thinking they were not going to succeed.

Materials can inspire the process.

Students may be stumped about how they are going to build a boat…until you show them that they can use clay. A parachute is daunting, but a pile of tissue paper or plastic bags might suddenly make students feel like they have some direction. On the other hand, materials can also instantly send the mind in certain directions, without exploring other options. For this reason, consider carefully the point at which you want to show students the materials they can use. You might want them to brainstorm materials first. This might inspire you to offer materials you had not considered before.

Some students or groups will need different types of support.

If possible, have students who need additional support manipulate materials, play with commercial solutions, or watch videos to get ideas. For students who need an additional challenge, consider ways to make the challenge more "real world" by adding additional realistic criteria. Or, encourage students to add their own criteria.

How to Use This Resource

Unit Structure Overview

This resource is organized into 12 units. Each three-week unit is organized in a consistent format for ease of use.

Week 1: STEAM Content

Day 1 Learn Content	Students read text, study visuals, and answer multiple-choice questions.
Day 2 Learn Content	Students read text, study visuals, and answer short-answer questions.
Day 3 Explore Content	Students engage in hands-on activities, such as scientific investigations, mini building challenges, and drawing and labeling diagrams.
Day 4 Get Creative	Students use their creativity, imaginations, and artistic abilities in activities such as drawing, creating fun designs, and doing science-related crafts.
Day 5 Analyze Data	Students analyze and/or create charts, tables, maps, and graphs.

Week 2: STEAM Challenge

Day 1 Understand the Challenge	Students are introduced to the STEAM Challenge. They review the criteria and constraints for successful designs.
Day 2 Research and Brainstorm	Students conduct additional research, as needed, and brainstorm ideas for their designs.
Day 3 Plan and Design	Students plan and sketch their designs.
Day 4 Build and Create	Students use their materials to construct their designs.
Day 5 Test and Evaluate	Students conduct tests and/or evaluation to assess the effectiveness of their designs and how well they met the criteria of the challenge.

Week 3: STEAM Challenge Improvement

Day 1 Reflect	Students answer questions to reflect on their first designs and make plans for how to improve their designs.
Day 2 Redesign	Students sketch new or modified designs.
Day 3 Rebuild and Refine	Students rebuild or adjust their designs.
Day 4 Retest	Students retest and evaluate their new designs.
Day 5 Reflect and Share	Students reflect on their experiences working through the engineering design process. They discuss and share their process and results with others.

How to Use This Resource *(cont.)*

Pacing Options

This resource is flexibly designed and can be used in tandem with a core curriculum within a science, STEAM, or STEM block. It can also be used in makerspaces, after-school programs, summer school, or as enrichment activities at home. The following pacing options show suggestions for how to use this book.

Option 1

This option shows how each unit can be completed in 15 days. This option requires approximately 10–20 minutes per day. Building days are flexible, and teachers may allow for additional time at their discretion.

	Day 1	Day 2	Day 3	Day 4	Day 5
Week 1	Learn Content	Learn Content	Explore Content	Get Creative	Analyze Data
Week 2	Understand the Challenge	Research and Brainstorm	Plan and Design	Build and Create	Test and Evaluate
Week 3	Reflect	Redesign	Rebuild and Refine	Retest	Reflect and Share

Option 2

This option shows how each unit can be completed in fewer than 15 days. This option requires approximately 45–60 minutes a day.

	Day 1	Day 2
Week 1	Learn Content Explore Content	Get Creative Analyze Data
Week 2	Understand the Challenge Research and Brainstorm Plan and Design	Build and Create Test and Evaluate
Week 3	Reflect Redesign Rebuild and Refine	Retest Reflect and Share

How to Use This Resource (cont.)

Teaching Support Pages

Each unit in this resource begins with two teaching support pages that provide instructional guidance.

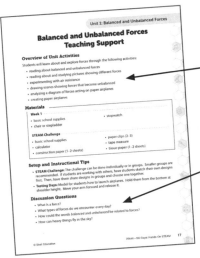

A clear overview of unit activities, weekly materials, safety notes, and setup tips help teachers plan and prepare efficiently and with ease.

Discussion questions help students verbalize their learning and connect it to their own lives.

Possible student misconceptions and design solutions help take the guesswork out of lesson planning.

Differentiation options offer ways to support and extend student learning.

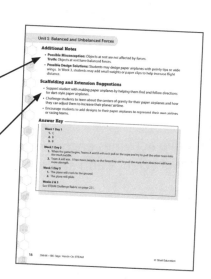

Materials

Due to the nature of engineering, the materials listed are often flexible. They may be substituted or added to, depending on what you have available. More material options require greater consideration by students and encourage more creative and critical thinking. Fewer material options can help narrow students' focus but may limit creativity. Adjust the materials provided to fit the needs of your students.

Approximate amounts of materials are included in each list. These amount suggestions are per group. Students are expected to have basic school supplies for each unit. These include paper, pencils, markers or crayons, glue, tape, and scissors.

How to Use This Resource *(cont.)*

Student Pages

Students begin each unit by learning about and exploring science-related content.

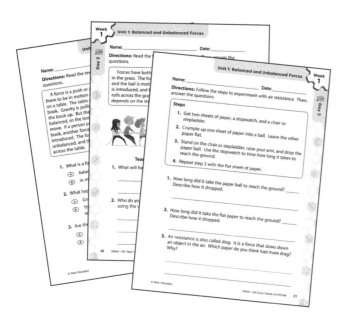

Activities in **Week 1** help build background science content knowledge relevant to the STEAM Challenge.

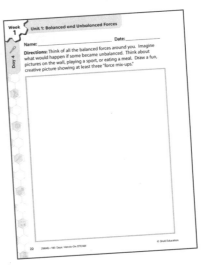

Creative activities encourage students to connect science and art.

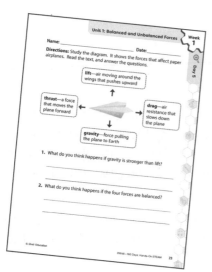

Graphs, charts, and maps guide students to make important mathematics and real-world connections.

How to Use This Resource *(cont.)*

Student Pages *(cont.)*

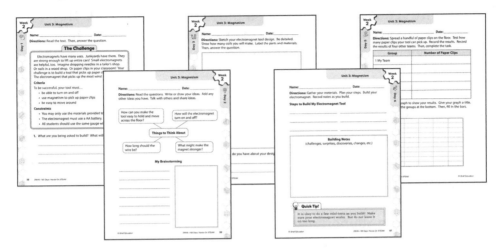

Week 2 introduces students to the STEAM Challenge. Activities guide students through each step of the engineering design process. They provide guiding questions and space for students to record their plans, progress, results, and thinking.

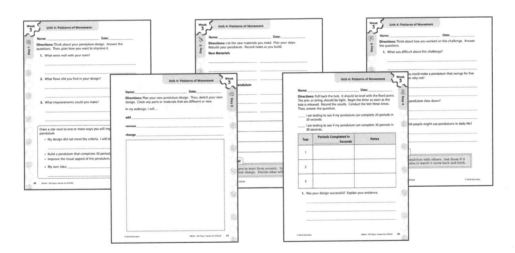

Week 3 activities continue to lead students through the cycle of the engineering design process. Students are encouraged to think about and discuss ways to improve their designs based on their observations and experiences in Week 2.

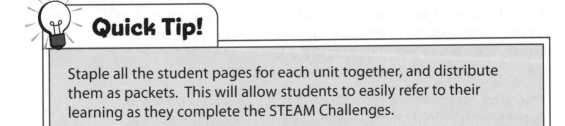

Quick Tip!

Staple all the student pages for each unit together, and distribute them as packets. This will allow students to easily refer to their learning as they complete the STEAM Challenges.

How to Use This Resource (cont.)

Assessment Options

Assessments guide instructional decisions and improve student learning. This resource offers balanced assessment opportunities. The assessments require students to think critically, respond to text-dependent questions, and utilize science and engineering practices.

Progress Monitoring

There are key points throughout each unit when valuable formative evaluations can be made. These evaluations can be based on group, paired, and/or individual discussions and activities.

- **Week 1** activities provide opportunities for students to answer multiple-choice and short-answer questions related to the content. Answer keys for these pages are provided in the Teaching Support pages.

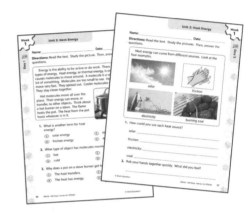

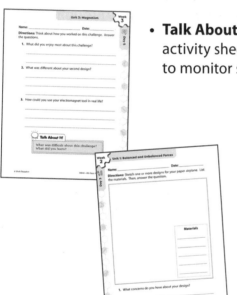

- **Talk About It!** graphics on student activity sheets offer opportunities to monitor student progress.

- **Week 2 Day 3: Plan and Design** is when students sketch their first designs. This is a great opportunity to assess how well students understand the STEAM challenge and what they plan to create. These should be reviewed before moving on to the Build and Create stages of the STEAM Challenges.

Summative Assessment

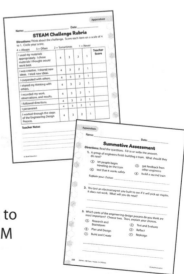

A rubric for the STEAM Challenges is provided on page 221. It is important to note that whether students' final designs were successful is not the main goal of this assessment. It is a way to assess students' skills as they work through the engineering design process. Students assess themselves first. Teachers can add notes to the assessment.

A short summative assessment is provided on page 222. This is meant to provide teachers with insight into how well students understand STEAM practices and the engineering design process.

Standards Correlations

Shell Education is committed to producing educational materials that are research and standards based. To support this effort, this resource is correlated to the academic standards of all 50 states, the District of Columbia, the Department of Defense Dependent Schools, and the Canadian provinces. A correlation is also provided for key professional educational organizations.

To print a customized correlation report for your state, visit our website at **www.tcmpub.com/ administrators/correlations** and follow the online directions. If you require assistance in printing correlation reports, please contact the Customer Service Department at 1-800-858-7339.

Standards Overview

The Every Student Succeeds Act (ESSA) mandates that all states adopt challenging academic standards that help students meet the goal of college and career readiness. While many states already adopted academic standards prior to ESSA, the act continues to hold states accountable for detailed and comprehensive standards. Standards are designed to focus instruction and guide adoption of curricula. They define the knowledge, skills, and content students should acquire at each level. Standards are also used to develop standardized tests to evaluate students' academic progress. State standards are used in the development of our resources, so educators can be assured they meet state academic requirements.

Next Generation Science Standards

This set of national standards aims to incorporate science knowledge and process standards into a cohesive framework. The standards listed on page 16 describe the science content and processes presented throughout the lessons.

TESOL and WIDA Standards

In this book, the following English language development standards are met: Standard 1: English language learners communicate for social and instructional purposes within the school setting. Standard 3: English language learners communicate information, ideas and concepts necessary for academic success in the content area of mathematics. Standard 4: English language learners communicate information, ideas and concepts necessary for academic success in the content area of science.

Standards Correlations (cont.)

Each unit in this resource supports all the following NGSS Scientific and Engineering Practices and Engineering Performance Expectations for 3–5.

Scientific and Engineering Practices	Engineering Performance Expectations
Asking Questions and Defining Problems	Define a simple design problem reflecting a need or a want that includes specified criteria for success and constraints on materials, time, or cost.
Developing and Using Models	
Planning and Carrying Out Investigations	
Analyzing and Interpreting Data	Generate and compare multiple possible solutions to a problem based on how well each is likely to meet the criteria and constraints of the problem.
Constructing Explanations and Designing Solutions	
Engaging in Argument from Evidence	Plan and carry out fair tests in which variables are controlled and failure points are considered to identify aspects of a model or prototype that can be improved.
Obtaining, Evaluating, and Communicating Information	

This chart shows how the units in this resource align to NGSS Disciplinary Core Ideas and Crosscutting Concepts.

Unit	Disciplinary Core Idea	Crosscutting Concept
Balanced and Unbalanced Forces	PS2.A: Forces and Motion PS2.B: Types of Interactions	Cause and Effect; Patterns
Heat Energy	PS3.B: Conservation of Energy and Energy Transfer	Energy and Matter
Magnetism	PS2.B: Types of Interactions	Cause and Effect
Patterns of Movement	PS2.A: Forces and Motion	Patterns
Adaptations	LS4.C: Adaptation	Cause and Effect
Animal Groups	LS2.D: Social Interactions and Group Behavior	Scale, Proportion, and Quantity
Changing Habitats	LS2.C: Ecosystem Dynamics, Functioning, and Resilience LS4.D: Biodiversity and Humans	Systems and System Models
Life Cycle of Plants	LS1.B: Growth and Development of Organisms LS1.A: Structure and Function	Systems and System Models; Patterns
Fossils	LS4.A: Evidence of Common Ancestry and Diversity	Scale, Proportion, and Quantity
Pollution Problems	ESS3.C: Human Impacts on Earth Systems	Systems and System Models
Severe Weather Hazards	ESS3.B: Natural Hazards ESS2.D: Weather and Climate	Cause and Effect; Patterns
Measuring the Weather	ESS2.D: Weather and Climate	Patterns

Balanced and Unbalanced Forces Teaching Support

Overview of Unit Activities

Students will learn about and explore forces through the following activities:

- reading about balanced and unbalanced forces
- reading about and studying pictures showing different forces
- experimenting with air resistance
- drawing scenes showing forces that become unbalanced
- analyzing a diagram of forces acting on paper airplanes
- creating paper airplanes

Materials Per Group

Week 1

- basic school supplies
- chair or stepladder
- stopwatch

STEAM Challenge

- basic school supplies
- calculator
- construction paper (1–2 sheets)
- paper clips (2–3)
- tape measure
- tissue paper (1–2 sheets)

Setup and Instructional Tips

- **STEAM Challenge:** The challenge can be done individually or in groups. Smaller groups are recommended. If students are working with others, have students sketch their own designs first. Then, have them share designs in groups and choose one together.
- **Testing Days:** Model for students how to launch airplanes. Hold them from the bottom at shoulder height. Move your arm forward and release it.

Discussion Questions

- What is a force?
- What types of forces do we encounter every day?
- How could the words *balanced* and *unbalanced* be related to forces?
- How can heavy things fly in the sky?

Additional Notes

- **Possible Misconception:** Objects at rest are not affected by forces.
  Truth: Objects at rest have balanced forces.
- **Possible Design Solutions:** Students may design paper airplanes with pointy tips or wide wings. In Week 3, students may add small weights or paper clips to help increase flight distance.

Scaffolding and Extension Suggestions

- Support student with making paper airplanes by helping them find and follow directions for dart-style paper airplanes.
- Challenge students to learn about the centers of gravity for their paper airplanes and how they can adjust them to increase their planes' airtime.
- Encourage students to add designs to their paper airplanes to represent their own airlines or racing teams.

Answer Key

Week 1 Day 1
1. C
2. B
3. B

Week 1 Day 2
1. When the game begins, Teams A and B will each pull on the rope and try to pull the other team into the mud puddle.
2. Team A will win. It has more people, so the force they use to pull the rope their direction will have more strength.

Week 1 Day 5
1. The plane will crash to the ground.
2. The plane will glide.

Weeks 2 & 3
See STEAM Challenge Rubric on page 221.

Name: _____ Date: _____

Directions: Read the text, and study the diagram. Then, answer the questions.

A force is a push or a pull. Forces act on objects and cause them to be in motion or stay at rest. Imagine a book sitting on a table. The table and gravity are both forces acting on the book. Gravity is pulling the book down; the table is pushing the book up. But the forces are balanced, so the book does not move. If a person pushes on the book, another force has been introduced. The forces are now unbalanced, and the book moves across the table.

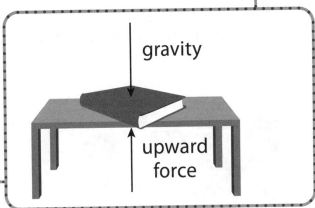

1. What is a force?

   Ⓐ balance or unbalance

   Ⓑ in motion or at rest

   Ⓒ a push or a pull

   Ⓓ action or inaction

2. What happens to an object with balanced forces?

   Ⓐ Gravity pulls it down.

   Ⓑ The object will stay at rest.

   Ⓒ The force will change direction.

   Ⓓ The object will move.

3. Are these forces balanced or unbalanced?

   Ⓐ balanced

   Ⓑ unbalanced

Name: _____   Date: _____

Directions: Read the text, and study the picture. Then, answer the questions.

> Forces have both strength and direction. Imagine a soccer ball in the grass. The forces of the ground and gravity are balanced, and the ball is motionless. If someone kicks the ball, a new force is introduced, and the forces become unbalanced. Now the ball rolls across the grass. How far will it go? Where will it go? That depends on the strength and direction of the kick.

Team A   **Team B**

1. What will happen when the tug-of-war game begins?

   _____

   _____

2. Who do you think will win the competition? Explain your answer using the words *force*, *strength*, and *direction*.

   _____

   _____

   _____

Name: _____ **Date:** _____

Directions: Follow the steps to experiment with air resistance. Then, answer the questions.

Steps

1. Get two sheets of paper, a stopwatch, and a chair or stepladder.

2. Crumple up one sheet of paper into a ball. Leave the other paper flat.

3. Stand on the chair or stepladder, raise your arm, and drop the paper ball. Use the stopwatch to time how long it takes to reach the ground.

4. Repeat step 3 with the flat sheet of paper.

1. How long did it take the paper ball to reach the ground? _____ Describe how it dropped.

_____

2. How long did it take the flat paper to reach the ground? _____ Describe how it dropped.

_____

3. Air resistance is also called *drag*. It is a force that slows down an object in the air. Which paper do you think had more drag? Why?

_____

_____

Day 4

Name: _____ Date: _____

Directions: Think of all the balanced forces around you. Imagine what would happen if some became unbalanced. Think about pictures on the wall, playing a sport, or eating a meal. Draw a fun, creative picture showing at least three "force mix-ups."

Name: _____ Date: _____

Directions: Study the diagram. It shows the forces that affect paper airplanes. Read the text, and answer the questions.

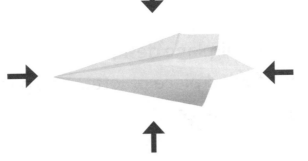

gravity—force pulling the plane to Earth

drag—air resistance that slows down the plane

thrust—a force that moves the plane forward

lift—air moving around the wings that pushes upward

1. What do you think happens if gravity is stronger than lift?

   _____

   _____

   _____

2. What do you think happens if the four forces are balanced?

   _____

   _____

   _____

Name: _____ Date: _____

Directions: Read the challenge. Then, answer the question.

The Challenge

Your class is having a paper airplane competition. You want to enter. Design and build a paper airplane that will fly the farthest distance.

Criteria

To be successful, your airplane design must…

- be made of a folded piece of letter-size paper.
- fly the farthest distance.

Constraints

- Paper is the only supply allowed.
- When each airplane is launched, it must be held in the same student's hand at shoulder-height.

1. What are you excited about?

_____

_____

 Quick Tip!

You will want to maximize thrust and lift. You will want to minimize drag and gravity.

Name: _____ **Date:** _____

Directions: Research three different types of paper airplanes. Record your findings in the table. Then, answer the questions.

Type of Plane	Sketch It	Describe It

1. Which type of plane do you think will travel the farthest? Why?

   _____

   _____

2. How do you think the wings will affect lift?

   _____

   _____

Name: _____ Date: _____

Directions: Sketch one or more designs for your paper airplane. Then, answer the question.

1. What concerns do you have about your design?

_____

_____

Name: _____ **Date:** _____

Directions: Read the questions to guide your planning. Build your paper airplane. Record notes as you build.

How can you make sure your paper airplane is symmetrical, or the same, on both sides?

What order should you follow to fold the paper?

Things to Consider

How will you maximize the distance the plane travels?

How can you practice for the competition?

Building Notes
(steps, challenges, discoveries, changes, etc.)

Quick Tip!

Make a few copies of your paper airplane design.
If you test one and it crashes, you will have backups.

Day 5

Name: _____ Date: _____

Directions: Hold the airplane at shoulder height. Hold it from the bottom to launch it. Test your paper airplane three times. Record the results. Then, answer the question.

Flight	Distance Traveled	Other Flight Notes
1		
2		
3		

Average distance: _____

Hint: To find the average distance, add up the times of all three flights. Then, divide that number by three. You may use a calculator.

1. Did your paper airplane travel the farthest distance?

   yes   no

2. If no, sketch what the airplane that did go the farthest looked like.

Name: _____ **Date:** _____

Directions: Think about your paper airplane design. Answer the questions. Then, plan how you want to improve it.

1. What went well with your paper airplane?

_____

_____

2. What could make your paper airplane even better?

_____

_____

_____

The following constraints have been adjusted.

- The airplane can be made of any type of paper.
- The paper can be any size.
- The airplane can include supplies other than paper.

3. How could the constraint changes help your design?

_____

_____

_____

Day 2

Name: _____ Date: _____

Directions: Plan your new paper airplane design. Then, sketch your new design. Label the materials. Then, complete the sentence.

In my redesign, I will…

add _____

change _____

1. This paper airplane design will work better because

_____

_____

Day 3

Name: _____ Date: _____

Directions: Gather your materials. Read the questions to guide your planning. Rebuild your paper airplane. Record notes as you build.

| What new materials do you need? | How do you need to change your steps? |

Things to Consider

| How many copies of this design will you make? | What adjustments will make it fly better? |

Building Notes
(steps, challenges, discoveries, etc.)

Quick Tip!

If your plane goes down fast, bend both sides of the tail up a little. Think of what other small changes might help.

Name: _____ Date: _____

Directions: Have one team member hold the airplane at shoulder height. They should hold the airplane at the bottom to launch it. Retest your paper airplane three times. Record the results.

Flight	Distance Traveled	Other Flight Notes
1		
2		
3		

Average distance: _____

Hint: To find the average distance, add up the times of all three flights. Then, divide that number by three. You may use a calculator.

1. Did your paper airplane travel the farthest distance?

yes   no

2. Did your new design work better? Explain your evidence.

yes   no

_____

_____

_____

Day 5

Name: _____ **Date:** _____

Directions: Think about how you worked on this challenge. Answer the questions.

1. What did you enjoy most about this challenge?

   _____

   _____

2. What did you learn from this challenge?

   _____

   _____

3. Which paper airplane design worked better? What made the difference?

   _____

   _____

4. What advice would you give to someone interested in making paper airplanes?

   _____

   _____

Talk About It!

What do you think engineers must consider when designing real planes?

Heat Energy Teaching Support

Overview of Unit Activities

Students will learn about and explore how heat energy is created and transferred through the following activities:

- reading about heat energy
- reading about and studying pictures of sources of heat energy
- experimenting with heat transfer and air pressure
- drawing imaginary hot and cold molecules
- analyzing a graph of changing water temperatures
- creating methods to cool water quickly

Materials Per Group

Week 1

- baking dish
- basic school supplies
- heat source and pot to boil water
- ice (3–4 cups, 1 L)

- pitcher
- plastic bottle with lid
- water (hot and cold)

STEAM Challenge

- basic school supplies
- cardboard [10-inch (25-cm) square]
- disposable plastic cup
- fabric (2–3 pieces)
- foil
- ice (cubes and crushed)
- paper bowl

- paper towels
- salt ($\frac{1}{2}$ cup, 135 g)
- thermometer
- variety of cups (thick/thin, plastic, glass, ceramic, etc.)
- water (room temperature)
- zip-top baggies (2)

Setup and Instructional Tips

- **Week 1 Day 3:** Use extreme caution when heating and pouring water in the bottle experiment. Only an adult should have access to the boiling water and heat source. This activity can also be done as a demonstration to save time and materials.

- **STEAM Challenge:** The challenge can be done individually or in groups. If students are working in groups, have students sketch their own designs first. Then, have them share designs in groups and choose one together.

- **Testing Days:** Because this challenge deals with cooling water, students should test their designs immediately after making them. Building and testing days should be done together.

Discussion Questions

- What is energy?
- Where does heat come from?
- Why do hot drinks cool off?
- How does technology help us cool things down and keep them cool?

Additional Notes

- **Possible Misconception:** Cold spreads to hot object.
  Truth: Heat transfers to colder objects. Hot objects lose heat.
- **Possible Design Solutions:** For Week 2, students might use crushed or whole ice. They might place cups of water in bowls filled with ice. They might test adding salt to the ice. Students might wrap cups in some sort of fabric or foam insulation, or use different types of cups.

Scaffolding and Extension Suggestions

- Ease the constraints by having students lower the water temperature by 10 degrees Fahrenheit instead of 20.
- Challenge students to read about the laws of thermodynamics.

Answer Key

Week 1 Day 1
1. C
2. A
3. A

Week 1 Day 2
1. solar: to dry wet clothes; friction: to warm your hands; electricity: to curl your hair; burning coal: to roast marshmallows
2. heat

Week 1 Day 5
1. The largest drop was between the beginning and five minutes.
2. The smallest drop was between 40 and 45 minutes.
3. The heat in the water was transferring to the air.
4. The water won't get below 72° because that is the temperature of the air of the room.

Weeks 2 & 3
See STEAM Challenge Rubric on page 221.

Name: _____ Date: _____

Directions: Read the text, and study the picture. Then, answer the questions.

Energy is the ability to be active or do work. There are different types of energy. Heat energy, or thermal energy, is one type. Heat causes molecules to move around. A molecule is a very small bit of something. Molecules are too small to see. Hot molecules move very fast. They spread out. Cooler molecules move slower. They stay closer together.

Hot molecules move all over the place. Their energy can move, or transfer, to other objects. Think about a hot burner on a stove. The flame heats the pot. The heat from the pot heats whatever is in it.

heat transfer

1. What is another term for heat energy?

   (A) solar energy   (C) thermal energy

   (B) friction energy   (D) molecule energy

2. What type of object has molecules moving quickly?

   (A) hot   (C) large

   (B) cold   (D) small

3. Why does a pot on a stove burner get hot?

   (A) The heat transfers.   (C) The pot creates heat.

   (B) The heat has energy.   (D) The pot's molecules move slowly.

Name: _____ **Date:** _____

Directions: Read the text, and study the pictures. Then, answer the questions.

Heat energy can come from different sources. Look at the four examples.

solar

friction

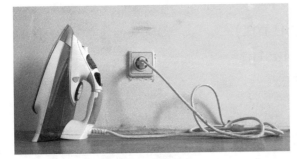

electricity

burning coal

1. How could you use each heat source?

solar: _____

friction: _____

electricity: _____

burning coal: _____

2. Rub your hands together quickly. What did you feel?

_____

Name: _____ Date: _____

Directions: Follow the steps to investigate heat transfer and air pressure.

Materials

baking dish	ice	water
plastic bottle with lid		pitcher

Steps

1. Fill the bottom of a baking dish with ice cubes. Fill a pitcher with ice and water.

2. Have an adult boil one cup (250 mL) of water and pour it into the plastic bottle. Let it sit for one minute. Then, screw on the lid.

3. Lay the bottle in the baking dish and pour the ice water over the top of the bottle.

4. Watch to see what happens!

What Happened?

The water and air molecules inside the bottle were very hot. They were moving quickly. Some were escaping out of the bottle. When the lid went on, the air molecules were trapped. Then came the sudden coldness of the ice and water. It quickly slowed down the molecules. They moved closer together. This made a negative vacuum. Crush! The walls of the bottle caved in.

Day 4

Name: _____ **Date:** _____

Directions: Heat can also be used to describe colors! Red, orange, and yellow are warm colors. Blue, green, and purple are cool. Use your imagination, and draw what warm and cool molecules might look like. Try to show their personalities, too.

Name: _____   Date: _____

Directions: Study the graph. Then, answer the questions.

Sam boiled one cup (250 mL) of water and poured it into a cup on the table. The temperature in the room was 72 °F (22 °C). She took the temperature of the water every five minutes for 45 minutes. She made a line graph to show the data.

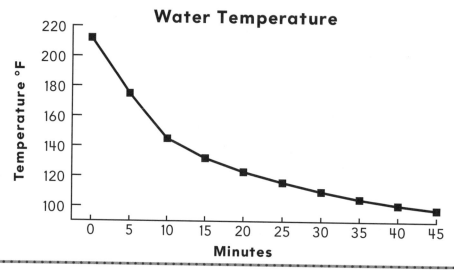

1. When was the largest drop in temperature? _____

2. When was the smallest drop in temperature? _____

3. Why was the temperature dropping? (Hint: Think about heat transfer!)

_____

_____

4. If Sam keeps the cup of water on the table, what is the lowest temperature it will reach? Why?

_____

_____

Name: _____ Date: _____

Directions: Read the text. Then, answer the questions.

The Challenge

On a hot day, a cold drink really hits the spot. But what if the water is just room temperature? It might not be as refreshing. You might want to cool it down quickly. Science can help! Your challenge is to create a system to lower the temperature of a cup of water. You want to do this as quickly as possible.

Criteria

To be successful, your water-cooling system must…

- lower the temperature of the water by 20 degrees Fahrenheit.
- lower the temperature in 5 minutes or less.

Constraints

- You may only use the materials provided to you.
- The water will be in a disposable plastic cup.

1. What questions do you have?

_____

_____

2. How would you explain the challenge in your own words?

_____

_____

Name: _____ Date: _____

Directions: Do some more research. Search for ways to cool water quickly. Answer the questions. Then, brainstorm some ideas. Write or draw as many ideas as you can. No idea is a bad idea!

1. How would you normally cool water?

_____

_____

2. What did your research teach you about cooling water?

_____

_____

Brainstorm Box

Quick Tip!

Research how salt can help cool water quickly.

Name: _____ Date: _____

Directions: Sketch your water-cooling system design. Label the parts. List the materials you will need.

Materials

_____   _____

_____   _____

_____   _____

Name: _____ **Date:** _____

Directions: Answer the questions. Gather your materials. Plan your steps. Make your rapid water-cooling system. Record notes in the box as needed.

1. What concerns do you have?

_____

_____

2. Make a prediction about how your plan will go.

_____

_____

Steps to Build My Water-Cooling System

_____

_____

_____

Building Notes
(additional steps, surprises, challenges, etc.)

Name: _____ **Date:** _____

Directions: Record the temperature of water before you pour it into your cup. Then, fill your cup with water. Place your thermometer in your cup of water. Record the temperature every minute for five minutes.

Time	Temperature (F)	Temperature (C)
beginning		
after 1 minute		
after 2 minutes		
after 3 minutes		
after 4 minutes		
after 5 minutes		

Total drop in temperature (in degrees Fahrenheit): _____

Name: _____ Date: _____

Directions: Think about your water-cooling system design. Answer the questions. Then, brainstorm how you can improve it.

1. What went well with your plan?

    _____

    _____

2. What flaws did you notice in your method?

    _____

    _____

The following criterion has been adjusted.

- Try to lower the temperature of the water by 30 degrees Fahrenheit in five minutes.

The following constraint has been adjusted.

- You may use a different type of cup to hold the water.

3. How could you make your water-cooling system design work better?

    _____

    _____

    _____

Name: _____ Date: _____

Directions: Plan your new water-cooling system design. Then, sketch your new design.

1. Will you put anything different in or around the water? Why or why not?

_____

_____

_____

2. Will you change anything about the cup? Why or why not?

_____

_____

_____

Name: _____ Date: _____

Directions: Answer the questions. Gather your materials. Plan your steps. Rebuild your water-cooling system. Record notes in the box as needed.

1. What predictions do you have about this new plan?

_____

_____

2. What new materials do you need?

_____

_____

Steps to Rebuild My Water-Cooling System

_____

_____

_____

_____

> **Building Notes**
> (additional steps, surprises, challenges, etc.)

Name: _____ **Date:** _____

Directions: Record the temperature of water before you pour it into your cup. Then, fill your cup with water. Place your thermometer in your cup of water. Record the temperature every minute for five minutes. Then, answer the questions.

Time	Temperature (F)	Temperature (C)
beginning (room temperature)		
after 1 minute		
after 2 minutes		
after 3 minutes		
after 4 minutes		
after 5 minutes		

Total drop in temperature (in degrees Fahrenheit): _____

1. Was your method successful? How do you know?

_____

_____

_____

Name: _____ Date: _____

Directions: Think about how you worked on this challenge. Answer the questions.

1. Did your second attempt to cool water work better? Explain your evidence.

_____

_____

_____

2. Draw yourself doing something you enjoyed during this challenge. Write a caption.

 Talk About It!

What did you learn from doing this challenge?

Magnetism Teaching Support

Overview of Unit Activities

Students will learn about and explore how and why magnets work through the following activities:

- reading about magnets
- reading about and studying images of maglev trains
- making compasses with sewing needles
- drawing comic strips of human magnets
- analyzing a diagram of an electromagnet
- creating electromagnets

Materials Per Group

Week 1

- bar magnet
- basic school supplies
- bowl of water
- compass (*optional*)
- sewing needle

STEAM Challenge

- basic school supplies
- batteries (AA, 9-volt, and a few other options if possible)
- cardboard tubes (1–2)
- copper wire, thinly coated (different gauges; available at craft and home improvement stores)
- craft sticks (3–5)
- electrical tape (*optional*)
- nails (different sizes; 2 each)
- paper clips or staples
- thick rubber bands (2)
- wooden dowels (3–4)

Setup and Instructional Tips

- **Week 1 Day 3:** Remind students to be careful when handling sewing needles.
- **STEAM Challenge:** The challenge can be done individually or in groups. If students are working in groups, have students sketch their own designs first. Then, have them share designs in groups and choose one together.
- **Building and Testing:** Instruct students to be responsible with the batteries and to be careful not to poke anything with the copper wire. Additionally, note that batteries will get hot quickly once all parts of the electromagnet are connected. Students should use tape or rubber bands to secure the wires and then hold batteries by their middles.

Discussion Questions

- What are magnets?
- Where have you seen magnets?
- How can magnets be used in real-world situations?

Additional Notes

- **Possible Misconception:** A magnet will pick up any metal object.
  Truth: Magnets attract iron objects or objects that contain some iron. Steel has some iron in it, so it is magnetic.

- **Possible Design Solutions:** Students may choose to use a heavier- or lighter-gauge copper wire. They may choose to wrap it around the nail many times or just a few. They might attach their electromagnets to the ends of sticks, or something similar, to move the tool easily.

Scaffolding and Extension Suggestions

- Allow students time to explore what magnets will or will not attract and to experience magnets repelling.

- Challenge students to learn how to create electromagnet trains by moving batteries through coiled wire.

Answer Key

Week 1 Day 1
1. D
2. A
3. B
4. C

Week 1 Day 2
1. A traveler might like maglev trains because they are faster and smoother.
2. The name *maglev* is short for magnetic levitation. They use magnets, which makes them levitate above the tracks.

Week 1 Day 5
1. battery
2. You can turn the electromagnet off by removing one end of the wire from the battery.
3. Turning off a magnet would be helpful if you needed to drop the object that was attracting to it.

Weeks 2 & 3
See STEAM Challenge Rubric on page 221.

Name: _____ Date: _____

Directions: Read the text, and study the picture. Then, answer the questions.

Magnetism is a force. A magnet is a type of metal that can pull some metal toward itself. A magnet can also push some metal away. If two magnets pull together, they attract. If they push apart, they repel. Magnets have a north and a south side. Opposite sides (north and south) will attract. Like sides (north and north or south and south) will repel.

1. Which of these objects could be magnetic?

   (A) wooden toothpick   (C) rubber band

   (B) piece of paper   (D) iron nail

2. Will these magnets attract or repel?

   (A) attract   (B) repel

3. Will these magnets attract or repel?

   (A) attract   (B) repel

4. Why is magnetism considered a force?

   (A) It attracts objects.   (C) It is a push or a pull.

   (B) It has a north and south side.   (D) It can be made of metal.

Day 2

Name: _____ Date: _____

Directions: Read the text, and study the diagram. Then, answer the questions.

> People want to get where they are going as fast as possible. Magnets can help! Maglev trains have repelling magnets on the tracks and the bottom of the trains. This allows them to zoom along tracks at very high speeds. *Maglev* is short for magnetic levitation. Levitation means to rise or hover in the air. Because the maglev trains do not touch the tracks, they appear to float. Most trains are on wheels that travel on tracks. They rub together, creating friction. Friction slows down the train. The strong magnets on maglev trains do not have any friction. These trains are fast and smooth.

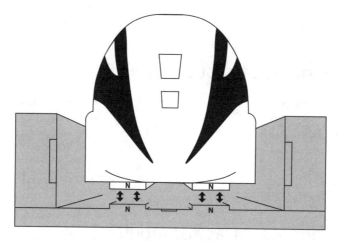

1. Why might a traveler prefer to ride a maglev train?

   _____

   _____

2. How do maglev trains get their name?

   _____

   _____

Name: _____ **Date:** _____

Directions: Read the text. Then, follow the steps to create a compass.

Earth is like a giant magnet. It has a north and a south pole just like a bar magnet. A compass is a device that always points to the North Pole. You can make a simple compass.

Materials

bar magnet	bowl of water	compass
scissors	sewing needle	thick paper

Make a Compass

1. Swipe the sewing needle up the bar magnet 50 times. Do not rub it back and forth. Each swipe should go from bottom to top.

2. Cut a circle out of the paper. It should be about 2 inches (5 cm) across. Fold the circle in half so it has a bend through the middle.

3. Lay the sewing needle in the bend of the circle.

4. Place the paper circle in a bowl of water. It will move around. Wait patiently until it straightens out. The needle will point north. Compare it to a compass.

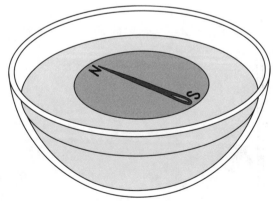

 Talk About It!

When or why would a compass be helpful?

Day 4

Name: _____ Date: _____

Directions: Magnets are usually made of metal. But, what if you were a magnet? Make a comic strip about you as a human magnet. What trouble might you have? How might you help others?

Name: _____ **Date:** _____

Directions: Study the diagram of an electromagnet. Then, answer the questions.

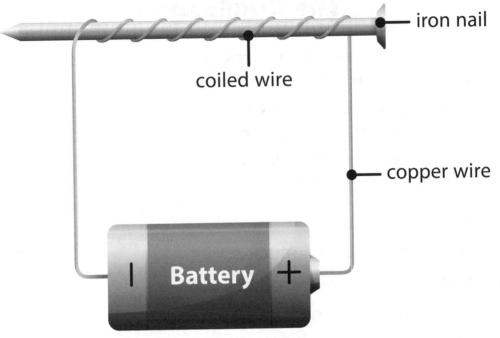

iron nail

coiled wire

copper wire

Battery

An electromagnet is a type of magnet. Its magnetic field is made by an electric current. Its magnetism can be turned on and off.

1. What part of the electromagnet supplies the electricity?

_____

2. How do you think you can turn the electromagnet on and off?

_____

_____

3. Why would it be helpful to be able to turn off a magnet?

_____

_____

Name: _____ Date: _____

Directions: Read the text. Then, answer the question.

The Challenge

Electromagnets have many uses. Junkyards have them. They are strong enough to lift up entire cars! Small electromagnets are helpful, too. Imagine dropping needles in a tailor's shop. Or nails in a wood shop. Or paper clips in your classroom! Your challenge is to build a tool that picks up paper clips or staples. The electromagnet that picks up the most wins!

Criteria

To be successful, your tool must…

- be able to turn on and off.
- use magnetism to pick up paper clips.
- be easy to move around.

Constraints

- You may only use the materials provided to you.
- The electromagnet must use a AA battery.
- All students should use the same gauge wire to start.

1. What are you being asked to build? What will be its purpose?

_____

_____

_____

Name: _____ **Date:** _____

Directions: Read the questions. Write or draw your ideas. Add any other ideas you have. Talk with others and share ideas.

How can you make the tool easy to hold and move across the floor?

How will the electromagnet turn on and off?

Things to Think About

How long should the wire be?

What might make the magnet stronger?

My Brainstorming

_____

_____

_____

_____

_____

_____

Day 3

Name: _____ Date: _____

Directions: Sketch your electromagnet tool design. Be detailed. Show how many coils you will make. Label the parts and materials. Then, answer the question.

1. What concerns do you have about your design?

_____

_____

Name: _____ Date: _____

Directions: Gather your materials. Plan your steps. Build your electromagnet. Record notes as you build.

Steps to Build My Electromagnet Tool

_____

_____

_____

Building Notes
(challenges, surprises, discoveries, changes, etc.)

 Quick Tip!

It is okay to do a few mini-tests as you build! Make sure your electromagnet works. But do not leave it on too long.

Day 5

Name: _____ Date: _____

Directions: Spread a handful of paper clips on the floor. Test how many paper clips your tool can pick up. Record the results. Record the results of four other teams. Then, complete the task.

Group	Number of Paper Clips
1 My Team	
2	
3	
4	
5	

Task: Create a bar graph to show your results. Give your graph a title. Write the names of the groups at the bottom. Then, fill in the bars.

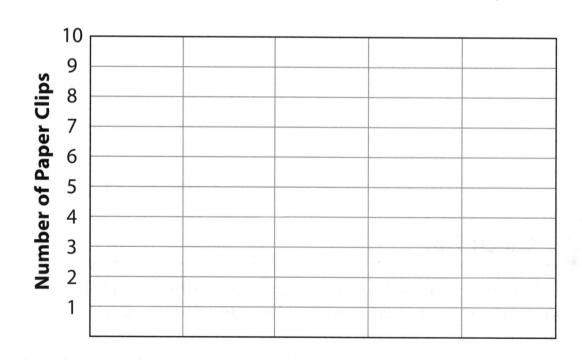

Name: _____ **Date:** _____

Directions: Think about your electromagnet tool. Answer the questions. Plan how you want to improve it.

1. What were some differences between electromagnet designs?

   _____

   _____

2. What seemed to help the electromagnets pick up more paper clips?

   _____

   _____

The following constraints have been adjusted. Consider these as you redesign your tool.

- You can use a different-size battery.
- You can use up to two batteries.
- You can use different gauges of wire.

3. How many paper clips do you want your new tool to pick up?

   _____

Name: _____ **Date:** _____

Directions: Plan your new electromagnet tool design. Sketch your new design. Label the parts and materials.

In my redesign, I will…

add _____

remove _____

change _____

1. Will you use any ideas you saw from others? Which ones?

_____

Name: _____ **Date:** _____

Directions: Gather your materials. Plan your steps. Rebuild your electromagnet. Record notes as you build.

Think About It!

What new materials do you need?
How do you need to change your steps?

Steps to Rebuild My Electromagnet Tool

_____

_____

_____

Building Notes
(additional steps, surprises, challenges, etc.)

Name: _____ Date: _____

Directions: Spread a handful of paper clips on the floor. Test how many paper clips your tool can pick up. Record the results. Record the results of four other teams. Then, answer the questions.

Group	Number of Paper Clips
1 My Team	
2	
3	
4	
5	

1. Does your new tool work better? What is your evidence?

yes   no

_____

_____

_____

Day 5

Name: _____ Date: _____

Directions: Think about how you worked on this challenge. Answer the questions.

1. What did you enjoy most about this challenge?

   _____

   _____

2. What was different about your second design?

   _____

   _____

   _____

3. How could you use your electromagnet tool in real life?

   _____

   _____

   _____

Talk About It!

What was difficult about this challenge?
What did you learn?

Patterns of Movement Teaching Support

Overview of Unit Activities

Students will learn about and explore patterns of movement through the following activities:

- reading about and studying pictures of patterns of movement
- reading about and studying pictures of zigzag movements
- making paintings with pendulums
- drawing pictures using patterns of movement
- analyzing a diagram of a pendulum
- creating pendulums

Materials Per Group

Week 1

- basic school supplies
- paint (with watery consistency; $\frac{1}{2}$ cup, 125 mL)
- paper or plastic cup

- plastic bag, tarp, or newspaper
- string (2 feet, 61 cm)

STEAM Challenge

- basic school supplies
- carboard square (5–10 inches, 13–25 cm)
- cardboard tubes (4–5)
- craft sticks (5–10)
- modeling clay

- pendulum bob options (block of wood, marble, golf ball, etc.)
- stopwatch
- string (2 feet, 61 cm)
- wooden dowels (5–10)

Setup and Instructional Tips

- **Week 1 Day 3:** Be sure to use washable, non-toxic paint during the pendulum painting. If necessary, put down a tarp or plastic bag to protect the painting surface.
- **STEAM Challenge:** The challenge can be done individually or in groups. If students are working in groups, have students sketch their own designs first. Then, have them share designs in groups and choose one together.

Discussion Questions

- What patterns do you notice in movement?
- How can understanding patterns in movement help you juggle?
- How does friction affect movement?
- What is a pendulum?
- How are pendulums used in everyday life?

Additional Notes

- **Possible Misconception:** My pendulum must complete one period each second for the challenge.
  Truth: The challenge is 20 periods completed in 20 seconds total. Friction will slow down the pendulum over time, so it will swing faster at the beginning of the 20 seconds and slower at the end.
- **Possible Design Solutions:** Students may choose different items as the pendulum bob. They may also create their own with modeling clay. Students might need to try different lengths of string and/or arms during their testing.

Scaffolding and Extension Suggestions

- Support students by showing them pictures or video clips of pendulums.
- Challenge students to build their pendulums to time accurately beyond 20 seconds.

Answer Key

Week 1 Day 1
   1. C
   2. A
   3. D

Week 1 Day 2
   1. They would go in a zigzag if they wanted to be cautious and go down slowly.
   2. A track athlete runs in a straight pattern.

Week 1 Day 5
   1. A golf ball would be better because it's heavier.
   2. A period is the amount of time it takes the pendulum to swing back and forth once.
   3. A short arm will have a shorter period because the bob will have a shorter distance to swing.

Weeks 2 & 3
See STEAM Challenge Rubric on page 221.

Name: _____ Date: _____

Directions: Read the text, and study the pictures. Then, answer the questions.

Objects with unbalanced forces are in motion. The motion can be irregular. Think of a leaf blowing in the wind. But motion often follows a pattern. It could be straight, like an arrow that has been shot. It could be circular, like a merry-go-round. Think of a girl jumping on a trampoline. She follows an up-and-down motion. Windshield wipers go back and forth. Friction is a force that slows down motion.

1. Which activity uses a circular pattern of motion?

   Ⓐ riding a pogo stick   Ⓒ jumping rope

   Ⓑ playing the piano   Ⓓ skiing down a hill

2. What slows down motion?

   Ⓐ friction   Ⓒ balanced forces

   Ⓑ patterns   Ⓓ unbalanced forces

3. What two patterns of motion would describe swinging?

   Ⓐ straight, back and   Ⓒ up and down, straight
       forth
                               Ⓓ up and down, back
   Ⓑ circular, up and down   and forth

Name: _____ Date: _____

Directions: Read the text, and study the pictures. Then, answer the questions.

Two patterns of movement are straight and zigzag. Motion in a straight line is fast. Think about a car driving on a straight road compared to a road that curves and winds around. It can go faster on the straight road. Motion in a zigzag is a little slower. Imagine a person standing on the top of a tall hill. Going straight down might be faster, but they would probably go down in a zigzag pattern. It might be slower, but it is safer.

1. Why might a skier go down in a zigzag pattern?

_____

_____

2. In what sport would an athlete run in a straight pattern? Explain your answer.

_____

_____

Name: _____ **Date:** _____

Directions: Read the text. Follow the steps to make art with a pendulum.

A pendulum has an object hung from a fixed point. The object can swing freely.

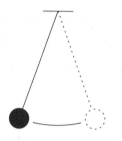

Materials

paint	paper
paper or plastic cup	string

Steps

1. Punch two holes on opposite sides at the top of a cup.

2. Poke a smaller hole in the bottom center of the cup. Cover it with tape.

3. Thread the string through the top holes. Tie a knot to look like a triangle.

4. Tape the other end of the string to the edge of a chair. Make sure the cup can swing freely.

5. Put paper beneath your pendulum cup.

6. Pour a little paint in the cup. Remove the tape from the bottom hole.

7. Gently pull the cup back and let it go. Try different patterns of movement, such as back-and-forth or circular.

Name: _____ **Date:** _____

Directions: Choose two patterns of motion from the list. Then, create a picture using only lines that follow those patterns.

> back and forth   circular   straight
>
> up and down   zigzag

Name: _____ Date: _____

Directions: Look at the diagram of a pendulum. Then, answer the questions.

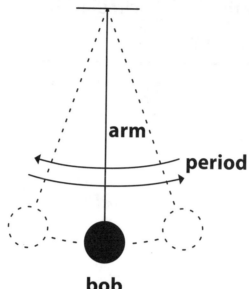

fixed point

arm

period

bob

1. Which do you think would swing for a longer time—a ping-pong ball or a golf ball? Why?

_____

_____

2. What is the period of a pendulum?

_____

_____

3. Would a short arm have a longer or shorter period? Explain your answer.

_____

_____

Day 1

Name: _____ Date: _____

Directions: Read the text. Then, answer the question.

The Challenge

Sometimes, life can be busy. School, sports, and chores can leave little time to relax. Deep breathing and meditation can help. Watching a pendulum swing back and forth can help, too. Some people have them on their desks. For this challenge, you will make a pendulum for your classroom. Then, students can take a pendulum break when they feel stressed. It might help improve their focus!

Criteria

To be successful, your pendulum must…

- have a bob, arm, and fixed point.
- complete 20 periods in 20 seconds.

Constraints

- You may only use the materials provided to you.

1. What questions do you have?

_____

_____

⭐ Try This!

If you want, make your own bob. Use modeling clay to shape it. What shape will work best? What shape will people enjoy watching?

Name: _____ Date: _____

Directions: Research pendulums. Search for ones made by other kids. Draw two examples you found. Then, answer the questions.

Pendulum 1	Pendulum 2

1. Search for information about the length of the arm. What did you learn?

_____

_____

2. Search for information about the weight and size of the bob. What did you learn?

_____

_____

3. What ideas do you have for your pendulum? Draw or write them.

Name: _____ Date: _____

Directions: Sketch two designs for your pendulum. Try to make them very different. Circle the one you like best. List the materials.

Design 1	Design 2

Materials

_____   _____

_____   _____

_____   _____

Name: _____ Date: _____

Directions: Gather your materials. Plan your steps. Build your pendulum. Read and think about the questions as you build and test your pendulum.

Steps to Build My Pendulum

_____

_____

_____

Are all the parts secure?

What changes can be made if the timing is off?

What would happen if you made the arm longer?

Things to Consider

How can you test the pendulum's swings?

Does the pendulum have enough room to swing freely?

Name: _____ **Date:** _____

Directions: Pull back the bob. It should be level with the fixed point. The arm, or string, should be tight. Begin the timer as soon as the bob is released. Record the results. Conduct the test three times. Then, answer the question.

Test	Periods Completed in 20 Seconds	Notes
1		
2		
3		

1. Was your design successful? What is your evidence?

_____

_____

_____

Name: _____ Date: _____

Directions: Think about your pendulum design. Answer the questions. Then, plan how you want to improve it.

1. What went well with your tests?

_____

_____

2. What flaws did you find in your design?

_____

_____

3. What improvements could you make?

_____

_____

Draw a star next to one or more ways you will improve your pendulum.

- My design did not meet the criteria. I will improve it by

_____

- Build a pendulum that completes 30 periods in 30 seconds.
- Improve the visual appeal of the pendulum.

- My own idea: _____

_____

Day 2

Name: _____ Date: _____

Directions: Plan your new pendulum design. Then, sketch your new design. Circle any parts or materials that are different or new.

In my redesign, I will…

add _____

remove _____

change _____

Name: _____ Date: _____

Directions: List the new materials you need. Plan your steps. Rebuild your pendulum. Record notes as you build.

New Materials

_____   _____

_____   _____

_____   _____

Steps to Build my Pendulum

_____

_____

_____

Building Notes

Problems	
Changes	
Surprises	

Quick Tip!

You do not have to start from scratch. You can adjust your first design. Decide what will work best.

Name: _____ **Date:** _____

Directions: Pull back the bob. It should be level with the fixed point. The arm, or string, should be tight. Begin the timer as soon as the bob is released. Record the results. Conduct the test three times. Then, answer the question.

_____ I am testing to see if my pendulum can complete 20 periods in 20 seconds.

_____ I am testing to see if my pendulum can complete 30 periods in 30 seconds.

Test	Periods Completed in _____ Seconds	Notes
1		
2		
3		

1. Was your design successful? Explain your evidence.

_____

_____

_____

Name: _____ **Date:** _____

Directions: Think about how you worked on this challenge. Answer the questions.

1. What was difficult about this challenge?

   _____

   _____

2. Do you think you could make a pendulum that swings for five minutes? Why or why not?

   _____

   _____

3. Why does your pendulum slow down?

   _____

   _____

4. How do you think people might use pendulums in daily life?

   _____

   _____

 Try This!

Share your pendulum with others. Ask them if it helps them relax to watch it move back and forth.

Adaptations Teaching Support

Overview of Unit Activities

Students will learn about and explore adaptations of plants and animals through the following activities:

- reading about animal and plant adaptations
- reading about and studying pictures of bird beak adaptations
- sculpting the head and beak of a new bird species
- drawing pictures of animals trying to adapt to new environments
- analyzing a graph of animals' swimming speeds
- creating insulation material

Materials Per Group

Week 1

- modeling clay

STEAM Challenge

- basic school supplies
- cotton balls (10+)
- craft feathers (small baggie full)
- duct tape
- felt or fabric
- foil
- ice water (3–4 cups, 1 L)
- packing peanuts (small baggie full)
- paper towels (5–10 sheets)
- shortening or vegetable oil (1 cup, 250 mL)
- thermometers (2)
- zip-top bags (small and large; 2+ each)

Setup and Instructional Tips

- **STEAM Challenge:** The challenge can be done individually or in groups. If students are working in groups, have students sketch their own designs first. Then, have them share designs in groups and choose one together.

Discussion Questions

- What are adaptations?
- What animals live in specific places? Why?
- How can animals survive in very hot or cold weather?
- What types of materials are used for insulation?

Additional Notes

- **Possible Misconception:** Animals can only live in one type of habitat.
  Truth: Wolves and foxes, for example, can live in both forest and tundra habitats, though the specific species have adaptations to live in each.
- **Possible Design Solutions:** Students might use shortening to imitate blubber, feathers for down, or fabric for fur. They should put one large zip-top bag inside another and fill the space between with insulating materials. They can close the top with duct tape.

Scaffolding and Extension Suggestions

- Review different habitats around the world and the special weather and conditions in each one. Brainstorm animals that live in each habitat.

Answer Key

Week 1 Day 1
1. C
2. D
3. B

Week 1 Day 2
1. Barn swallows cannot survive winters. It is too cold and there isn't enough food, so they go south where it is warmer.
2. Other animals will leave the milk snakes alone.

Week 1 Day 5
1. 15 mph (25 km/h)
2. Swimming fast is an adaptation because it is something that can help an animal live in its ocean or sea habitat.
3. A penguin could not swim away from a predator in the water because it is not a very fast swimmer.

Weeks 2 & 3
See STEAM Challenge Rubric on page 221.

Name: _____ **Date:** _____

Directions: Read the text, and study the picture. Then, answer the questions.

Many plants and animals have adaptations. These are traits that help them live in certain places.

The roots of a cactus help it live in the desert. The roots are shallow. They can quickly absorb water when it rains. Grasses in the prairie survive because of their deep roots. The roots reach water far beneath the ground.

Animals also have adaptations. A leopard's fur coat has spots. This helps it blend in, or camouflage. A penguin has a thick layer of fat called blubber. The blubber keeps it warm. Without special adaptations, many living things would not survive.

1. A trait that helps an animal live in a certain place is _____.

   Ⓐ a shallow root
   Ⓒ an adaptation
   Ⓑ blubber
   Ⓓ camouflage fur

2. What is blubber?

   Ⓐ deep roots
   Ⓒ spotted fur
   Ⓑ an animal living in cold weather
   Ⓓ a layer of fat

3. Which adaptation is an example of camouflage?

   Ⓐ A fish has gills to breathe underwater.
   Ⓒ A desert fox has big ears to help it cool down.
   Ⓑ A butterfly blends in to a plant leaf.
   Ⓓ A bird flies to warmer climates when it is cold.

Unit 5: Adaptations

Name: _____ Date: _____

Directions: Read about different types of adaptations. Study the pictures. Then, answer the questions.

Camouflage	Mimicry
Peppered moths are white with black marks. They blend in perfectly with tree trunks and branches.	Milk snakes are harmless. But they look like venomous copperheads.
Hibernation	**Migration**
When black bears hibernate, their bodies use less energy. They live off stored layers of fat.	Barn swallows live in North America during warm seasons. They fly to South America when it is cold.

1. Why would barn swallows fly south for winter?

_____

2. Why would looking like a copperhead snake help milk snakes survive?

_____

Day 3

Name: _____ **Date:** _____

Directions: Birds' beaks are great examples of adaptations. Study the different types of beaks. Discuss how the beaks might be helpful adaptations. Then, complete the task.

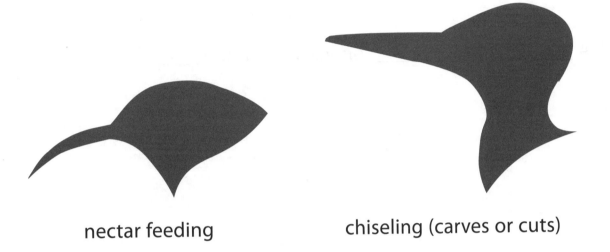

nectar feeding

chiseling (carves or cuts)

dip netting

seed eating

Task: Create a new species of bird. Think about what the bird will do, where it will live, and how it will eat. Decide what its beak should look like so it can survive. Use clay to form its head and beak. Share your new bird with a partner. See if they can guess how it uses its beak.

Name: _____ Date:_____

Directions: Imagine an animal is visiting a new and different habitat. What would the animal need to do or wear to survive? Draw an animal on vacation in the wrong place. Be creative! Would the animal need a winter coat or a life jacket? Use your imagination, and have fun!

A _____ on vacation in the _____.

Name: _____ Date: _____

Directions: Study the bar graph comparing swimming speeds of animals. Then, answer the questions.

Fast Swimmers

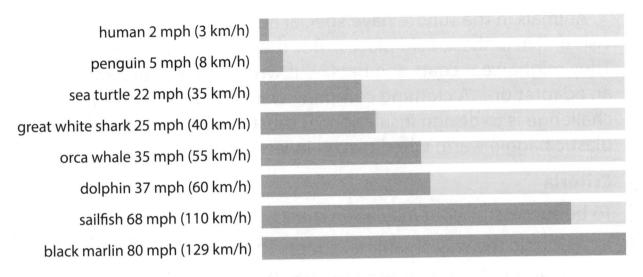

human 2 mph (3 km/h)
penguin 5 mph (8 km/h)
sea turtle 22 mph (35 km/h)
great white shark 25 mph (40 km/h)
orca whale 35 mph (55 km/h)
dolphin 37 mph (60 km/h)
sailfish 68 mph (110 km/h)
black marlin 80 mph (129 km/h)

1. How much faster is a dolphin than a sea turtle?

_____

2. Why would an animal's swimming speed be a helpful adaptation?

_____

_____

3. Do you think a penguin could swim away from a predator in the water? Why or why not?

_____

_____

_____

Name: _____ Date: _____

Directions: Read the text. Then, answer the questions.

The Challenge

Animals in the tundra have special adaptations. People can visit or live in these cold places. But they need to be prepared. They might wear coats and hats. But what if they could imitate an adaptation? A clothing company wants your help. Your challenge is to design insulation. It must keep the inside of a plastic baggie warm when placed in ice water.

Criteria

To be successful, your insulation must...

- mimic the way an animal adapts to the cold.
- stay within 15 degrees Fahrenheit of the starting temperature after 5 minutes.

Constraints

- You may only use the materials provided to you.

1. What are you being asked to design?

_____

_____

2. How will you know your design is successful?

_____

_____

Name: _____ **Date:** _____

Directions: Research three arctic or antarctic animals. Then, answer the questions.

1. Animal: _____

Adaptations for warmth: _____

_____

2. Animal: _____

Adaptations for warmth: _____

_____

3. Animal: _____

Adaptations for warmth: _____

_____

💡 **Quick Tip!**

To set up your design, put a large plastic zip-top bag inside another one. The space between the two baggies can be for your insulation. The innermost part is where the thermometer will go.

Name: _____ Date: _____

Directions: Sketch a design for your insulation. Be as detailed as you can. Label all the materials. Show where the materials will go.

 Think About It!

Should you seal the top of your insulation? How?

Name: _____ Date: _____

Directions: List and gather your materials. Plan your steps. Make your insulation. Record notes as you build.

Materials

_____   _____

_____   _____

_____   _____

Steps to Build My Insulation

_____

_____

_____

Building Notes
(problems, solutions, changes, etc.)

Name: _____ Date: _____

Directions: Place a thermometer inside your insulated bag. Place a thermometer inside a plain plastic bag. Record the starting temperatures. Then, place both bags in a bowl of ice water. Wait five minutes. Record the results. Then, answer the questions.

	Fahrenheit	**Celsius**
starting temperature inside bags		
temperature inside insulated bag after 5 minutes		
temperature inside plain bag after 5 minutes		

1. What is the difference in temperature between the inside of the insulated bag and the plain bag?

   _____ (Fahrenheit)   _____ (Celsius)

2. Was your insulation design successful? What is your evidence?

   _____

   _____

   _____

Name: _____ Date: _____

Directions: Think about your insulation design. Answer the questions. Then, plan how you want to improve it.

1. What do you think worked well with your insulation?

_____

_____

2. How could you make the insulation work better?

_____

_____

Was your first design successful? If so, you can still improve it. Set a new goal.

My new insulation will keep the temperature within

_____ degrees of the starting temperature.

Day 2

Name: _____ **Date:** _____

Directions: Plan your new design. Then, sketch your new insulation bag. Label all the materials. Then, complete the sentence.

In my redesign, I will…

add _____

remove _____

change _____

1. This insulation will work better because _____

_____

Day 3

Name: _____ **Date:** _____

Directions: List and gather your materials. Plan your steps. Make your new insulation. Record notes as you build.

Materials

_____   _____

_____   _____

_____   _____

Steps to Build My Insulation

_____

_____

_____

| **Building Notes** |
| (problems, solutions, changes, etc.) |
| |

Day 4

Name: _____ **Date:** _____

Directions: Place a thermometer inside your insulated bag. Place a thermometer inside a plain plastic bag. Record the starting temperatures. Then, place both bags in a bowl of ice water. Wait five minutes. Record the results. Then, answer the questions.

	Fahrenheit	**Celsius**
starting temperature inside bags		
temperature inside insulated bag after 5 minutes		
temperature inside plain bag after 5 minutes		

1. What is the difference in temperature between the inside of the insulated bag and the plain bag?

   _____ (Fahrenheit)   _____ (Celsius)

2. Did your new insulation design work better? What is your evidence?

   _____

   _____

   _____

© Shell Education

Name: _____ **Date:** _____

Directions: Think about how you worked on this challenge. Answer the questions.

1. Do you think the clothing company would approve your design? Explain your answer.

   _____

   _____

2. What types of clothing could your insulation be used in?

   _____

   _____

3. What do you wish you had done differently?

   _____

   _____

4. Draw yourself working as an engineer in this challenge. Write a caption.

   ┌──┐
   │   │
   │   │
   │   │
   │   │
   │   │
   │   │
   │   │
   └──┘

Animal Groups Teaching Support

Overview of Unit Activities

Students will learn about and explore why some animals live in groups through the following activities:

- reading about animals that live in groups
- reading about whale pods
- working in groups to create tall structures
- drawing family portraits
- analyzing a map of flamingo populations
- creating cooperative games

Materials Per Group

Week 1

- dry spaghetti noodles (1 package)
- mini-marshmallows (20+)

STEAM Challenge

- basic school supplies
- game component pieces (dice, cards, buttons, etc.)
- posterboard

Setup and Instructional Tips

- **STEAM Challenge:** The challenge can be done individually or in groups. Groups are recommended to support the content of this unit. If students are working in groups, have students sketch their own designs first. Then, have them share designs in groups and choose one together.

Discussion Questions

- Do humans live their lives alone or with other people? Why?
- Why would animals live in groups?
- What advantages or disadvantages are there to living in groups?
- What advantages or disadvantages are there to living alone?
- What character traits do people need to work and thrive in groups?

Additional Notes

- **Possible Design Solutions:** Students might need guidance to develop the general concept for their games. They need to have a clear objective (how to win as a group) and parameters (to know if they win). Time limits and setting a number of turns are examples.

Scaffolding and Extension Suggestions

- Support students by helping them find examples of cooperative kids' games and discussing the rules and objectives of the games.

- Encourage students to learn about specific jobs that can be assigned to individual members of animal groups.

Answer Key

Week 1 Day 1
1. C
2. D
3. A

Week 1 Day 2
1. The whales have some sort of plan to hunt that will trick their prey.
2. Killer whales hunt and play together.
3. Answers should state a favorite fact about killer whales.

Week 1 Day 5
1. Antarctica, Australia
2. Flamingos live along coasts. They live closer to the equator than the poles.
3. Answer should state a location that students would travel to see flamingos.

Weeks 2 & 3
See STEAM Challenge Rubric on page 221.

Name: _____ **Date:** _____

Directions: Read the text, and study the picture. Then, answer the questions.

Animals all over the world live in different ways. Some adult animals, such as bears, skunks, and koalas, live alone. Others, such as wolves, crows, and bees, live in groups. Living in groups can have benefits. There are more animals to hunt or find food. They can protect each other and help care for the young. Older animals can teach the younger ones. Sometimes, animals in groups have specific jobs. Animal groups can have fun names. A group of meerkats is called a mob. A group of baboons is called a troop.

1. What is one reason some animals live in groups?

   Ⓐ to rely on their instincts

   Ⓑ to hunt in new places

   Ⓒ to be protected by others

   Ⓓ to go wherever they want

2. Which adult animal lives alone?

   Ⓐ wolf

   Ⓑ crow

   Ⓒ bee

   Ⓓ bear

3. What might be a disadvantage of living in a group?

   Ⓐ They might have a shortage of food.

   Ⓑ They might teach the younger animals.

   Ⓒ They might protect each other.

   Ⓓ They might have their own jobs.

Name: _____ **Date:** _____

Directions: Read the text. Then, answer the questions.

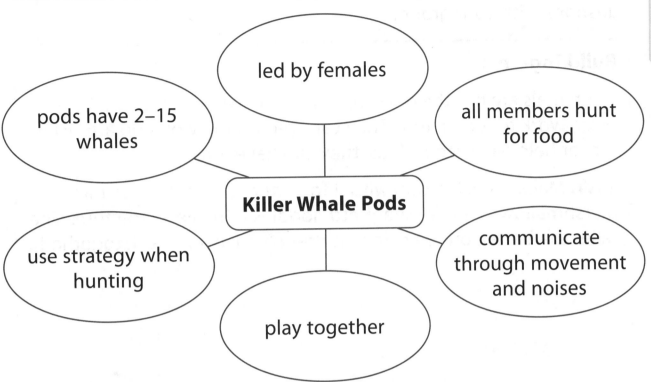

1. What do you think it means that whales use *strategy* to hunt?

_____

_____

2. What do killer whales do together?

_____

_____

3. Which fact did you find most interesting? Why?

_____

_____

Name: _____ Date: _____

Directions: Read the text, and complete the task. Then, discuss the questions with your group.

Build Together

Animals are not the only creatures who work in groups. People often work together, too. They can split up the work, do a specific job, or help each other. Plus, they can have fun!

Task: Make a small group with 2 to 3 other students. Use mini-marshmallows and dry spaghetti noodles to make a structure. The taller the better, but be careful it doesn't fall over. Work together!

Discussion Questions

1. How was your group similar to a group of animals working together? How was it different?

2. What was good about working together? What was hard?

3. What problems might animals have when they live and work in groups?

4. Would this activity be easier to do by yourself or with a group? Why?

5. Would this activity be easier to do with a larger group? Why?

Name: _____ **Date:** _____

Directions: Humans live in groups, too! Draw your family.
Sometimes, close friends are like family. Add them, too, if you want.
Label each person with their name and a job they do to help the
group.

Name: _____ Date: _____

Directions: Read the text, and study the map. Then, answer the questions.

A group of flamingos is called a flamboyance. Some groups have only 50 birds. Others have thousands! Flamingos put their heads down to eat. Staying in a group helps keep them safe from predators.

Flamingos in the Wild

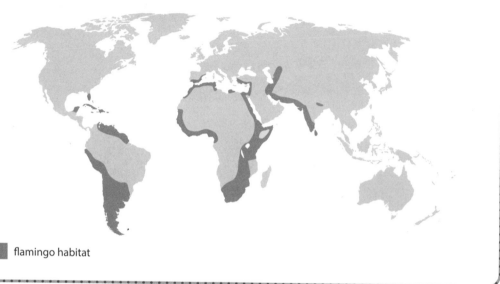

flamingo habitat

1. Name one continent where flamingos do not live.

_____

2. In general, where do flamingos like to live?

_____

3. Where would you want to go to observe a flamboyance of flamingos? Why?

_____

_____

Name: _____ Date: _____

Directions: Read the text. Then, explain the challenge in your own words to someone else.

The Challenge

A toy store wants you design a game to show how animals work together. You must create a cooperative board game. In this type of game, players work together to achieve a goal. They do not compete against each other. Just like animal groups! Make your game fun to play and challenging to win.

Criteria

To be successful, your cooperative game must…

- have clear directions, including a goal, or objective.
- be about an animal group trying to accomplish something.
- be playable by three or more students.

Constraints

- You may only use the materials provided to you.

Quick Tip!

Think of a goal for your game. Maybe it is to find food or shelter. Or it might be to rescue an injured group member or escape predators. When you know the goal, decide how players will know if they won. For example, you could have a time limit or set a maximum number of turns to reach the goal.

Name: _____ Date: _____

Directions: Choose an animal group to base your game on. Circle your choice. Research the animal group. Answer the questions. Then, brainstorm your ideas.

Animals That Live in Groups

ants	bees	crows
deer	dolphins	elephants
gorillas	lions	meerkats
penguins	prarie dogs	red foxes
wolves	zebra	other: _____

---

1. What is a group of these animals called? _____

2. Where do these animals live? _____

3. How many animals are in a typical group? _____

4. Write a few sentences about what else you learned. What do the groups do? What roles are there in the group?

_____

_____

_____

5. What could be the goal, or objective, of your game? Write as many ideas as you can.

_____

_____

Name: _____ **Date:** _____

Directions: Sketch a design for your cooperative board game. Sketch any parts or pieces that go with it. Then, complete the sentences.

The goal of the game is to _____

Players will move on the board by (*circle one*)

     rolling dice   pulling cards   flicking a spinner

     other: _____

Name: _____ Date: _____

Directions: Gather your materials. Plan the jobs each person in your group will do. Build your cooperative board game. Then, write the directions for your game.

Cooperative Board Game Group Plan

	Job or Task	Group Member(s)
1		
2		
3		
4		
5		
6		

Game Directions

_____

_____

_____

_____

_____

_____

Name: _____ Date: _____

Directions: Give your game to another group to play. When they are finished, have them complete the survey.

1. Did you understand the directions?

yes   sort of   no

2. Did you enjoy playing the game?

very much   sort of   not much

3. What did you learn about the animal group the game was based on?

_____

_____

_____

4. What did you like best about the game?

_____

_____

_____

5. What suggestions do you have to make the game even better?

_____

_____

_____

Name: _____ Date: _____

Directions: Think about your cooperative game board design. Answer the questions. Then, plan how you want to improve it.

1. What do you like best about your design?

   _____

   _____

2. What do you think needs to be better?

   _____

   _____

3. What did you like best about the group's game that you tested and played?

   _____

   _____

   _____

Look carefully at the feedback from the students that played your game. Use their comments to plan improvements.

In response to feedback, we will improve our game by

_____

_____

Day 2

Name: _____ Date: _____

Directions: Plan your new cooperative board game design. Then, sketch your new design.

1. Do you need to change the game's objective? If so, what is the new one?

_____

_____

2. Do you need to update the directions? How?

_____

_____

3. What other changes will you make?

_____

_____

Name: _____ Date: _____

Directions: Gather your materials. Plan the jobs each person in your group will do. Rebuild your cooperative board game. Then, write the revised directions for your game.

Cooperative Board Game Group Plan

	Job or Task	Group Member(s)
1		
2		
3		
4		
5		
6		

Game Directions

_____

_____

_____

_____

_____

_____

Name: _____ **Date:** _____

Directions: Give your game to the same group to play. When they are finished, have them complete the survey.

1. Did you understand the directions?

   yes   sort of   no

2. Did you enjoy playing the game?

   very much!   sort of   not much

3. What did you learn about the animal group the game was based on?

   _____

   _____

4. What problems were fixed from the first time you played the game?

   _____

   _____

5. What compliments could you give to the creators of this game?

   _____

   _____

   _____

   _____

Name: _____ **Date:** _____

Directions: Think about how you worked on this challenge. Answer the questions.

1. What challenges did you have making the game?

   _____

   _____

2. What did you enjoy about making the game?

   _____

   _____

3. Do you like cooperative games or traditional competition games better? Why?

   _____

   _____

   _____

4. What advice would you give to other game designers?

   _____

   _____

   _____

Changing Habitats Teaching Support

Overview of Unit Activities

Students will learn about and explore the causes and effects of changes to habitats through the following activities:

- reading about different causes of habitat changes
- reading about and studying a chart about invasive species
- making paper plate dioramas to show solutions to habitat changes
- drawing signs to help protect habitats
- analyzing a table of wildfire data
- creating animal crossing bridges

Materials Per Group

Week 1

- basic school supplies
- construction paper

- paper plate

STEAM Challenge

- apple
- basic school supplies
- cardboard tubes (4–6)
- clothespins (5–10)
- cotton swabs (10–20)
- pipe cleaners (5–10)

- ruler
- straws (5–10)
- string (3+ feet, 1+ meter)
- wood supplies (craft sticks, pencils, dowels, etc.; 10–15 of each)
- yarn (3+ feet, 1+ meter)

Setup and Instructional Tips

- **STEAM Challenge:** The challenge can be done individually or in groups. If students are working in groups, have students sketch their own designs first. Then, have them share designs in groups and choose one together.

Discussion Questions

- How do habitats change over time?
- Are habitat changes always bad? Why or why not?
- How do habitat changes affect wildlife and people?
- What can be done to prevent or repair negative habitat changes?

Additional Notes

- **Possible Misconception:** People are the only cause of habitat changes.
  Truth: Weather, natural disasters, fire, and other animals can also cause changes.

- **Possible Design Solutions:** Students will need to find or create supports on both ends of their bridges. For example, they might have bridges that connect two chairs or tables. The string might cross back and forth or have straws or sticks along it to provide steps.

Scaffolding and Extension Suggestions

- Support students by helping them find and watch videos about building simple rope bridges and let them copy the method.

- Challenge students to investigate any habitat changes in their own communities and their effects.

Answer Key

Week 1 Day 1
1. A
2. C
3. D

Week 1 Day 2
1. European Starling
2. Asian carp

Week 1 Day 5
1. 2020
2. 2019
3. The year 2020 might have had the worst drought because dry forests burn easier.
4. Wildfires can destroy plants and trees, which animals use for shelter. Wildfires could kill animals that are food for other animals.

Weeks 2 & 3
See STEAM Challenge Rubric on page 221.

Name: _____ Date: _____

Directions: Read the text, and study the picture. Then, answer the questions.

Habitats can change with time. There are many reasons for this. Weather is one of them. Droughts can cause changes. So can excess rain. Natural disasters, such as hurricanes and earthquakes, can also cause change. Animals can even change their own habitats. Beavers build dams. This can change a river's route. Invasive species can cause problems. These animals are not native to a habitat. People can change habitats. They might cut down trees to make space to build. Pollution might also change habitats. It can become unsafe for wildlife to live there.

1. Which cause of habitat change is *not* a natural disaster?

   Ⓐ pollution

   Ⓑ earthquake

   Ⓒ volcano

   Ⓓ hurricane

2. What is an invasive species?

   Ⓐ An animal that changes a river's route.

   Ⓑ An animal that changes a habitat.

   Ⓒ An animal that is not native to an area.

   Ⓓ An animal that helps a habitat become better.

3. Which activity is an example of animals changing their habitat?

   Ⓐ Birds lay eggs in nests.

   Ⓑ Fish blend in with their surroundings.

   Ⓒ Lions sleep under trees.

   Ⓓ Woodpeckers make holes in trees.

Day 2

Name: _____ Date: _____

Directions: Read the text, and study the chart. Then, answer the questions.

An invasive species can be plants or animals. They are brought to a new habitat. They can upset the balance in a place. An invasive animal might overhunt. An invasive plant might grow too big. These changes can hurt the plants and animals who belong there.

Comparing Invasive Species in the U.S.

	Burmese Python	**European Starling**	**Asian Carp**
Native To	Asia	Europe, Africa, Asia	Asia
Year Found in the U.S.	2000	1890	1970s
Reason They Were Brought to the U.S.	for exotic pet trading	because they were mentioned in a famous play	to help keep fish farms clean
Negative Effects	They overhunt small and medium-size mammals, which disrupts the food web.	They live in very large groups and destroy crops.	They compete with native fish for food and space.

1. Which invasive species has been in the U.S. the longest?

_____

2. Which species was brought to try and help a habitat?

_____

Name: _____ Date: _____

Directions: Read about different habitat changes that could happen. Choose one situation. Create a diorama, using a paper plate and art supplies, that shows a possible solution.

The Desert	**The Rain Forest**
A group of lizards in the desert use the same water hole. After a summer of no rain, the water hole has dried up. What can the lizards do?	A group of toucans nest in a cluster of trees in the rain forest. The trees are cut down by people. What should the toucans do?

The River	**The Swamp**
A group of trout swim a river route every year. Beavers move to the forest and build a dam, blocking the river. What should the trout do?	A group of egrets eat the small animals that live in the water. An invasive species eats a lot of the aquatic animals. What should the egrets do?

Day 4

Name: _____ Date: _____

Directions: People can change habitats in negative ways. Create a sign to encourage people to be careful and responsible so habitats stay safe.

Name: _____ Date: _____

Directions: Read the text, and study the table. Then, answer the questions.

Droughts create dry forest conditions. This means wildfires can begin easily and spread quickly. This table shows how many acres of land were burned by wildfires in California.

California Wildfires

Year	Land Burned
2015	880,000 acres
2016	670,000 acres
2017	1,500,000 acres
2018	1,900,000 acres
2019	260,000 acres
2020	4,200,000 acres

1. In which year did the most acres burn? _____

2. In which year did the fewest acres burn? _____

3. Which year do you think had the worst drought? Why?

   _____

   _____

4. What are two ways wildfires could affect habitats?

   _____

   _____

Name: _____ **Date:** _____

Directions: Read the text. Then, answer the questions.

The Challenge

Each year, trees are cut down to make space for new roads. Squirrels and other small animals do not have safe ways to get across. Some cities have started building wildlife crossways. These bridges allow animals to move from place to place safely.

For this challenge, you must build a model of an animal rope bridge. Then, squirrels can use them to travel across a road.

Criteria

To be successful, your bridge must…

- create a crossing between two things, such as chairs or tables. These represent trees.
- support a large apple without falling. The apple represents a squirrel.
- be at least 18 inches (46 cm) in length.

Constraints

- You may only use the materials provided to you.
- The bridge may not have any support in the middle, just on each end.

1. What are you being asked to build?

_____

2. What questions do you have?

_____

_____

Name: _____ **Date:** _____

Directions: Research animal rope bridges. Find some examples. Answer the questions.

1. What are three facts you learned about animal bridges?

_____

_____

_____

2. Draw two examples of animal rope bridges.

3. Where will you attach each end of your bridge?

_____

4. What other ideas do you have? Write or draw as many as you can.

Name: _____ Date: _____

Directions: Sketch two designs for your animal rope bridge. Try to make them very different. Circle what you like best in each one. Use those ideas to sketch a third design. Label the materials.

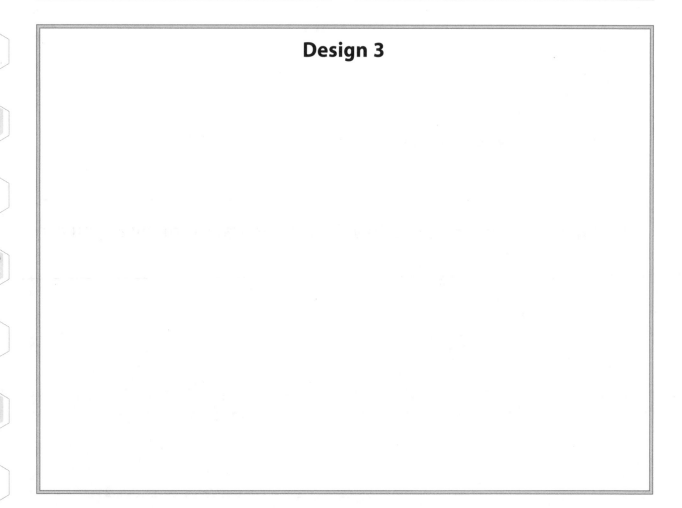

Design 1

Design 2

Design 3

Name: _____ Date: _____

Directions: Gather your materials, and plan your steps. Build your rope bridge. Record notes as you build.

Steps to Build My Animal Rope Bridge

_____

_____

_____

_____

Building Notes

Problems	
Changes	
Other Notes	

Name: _____ **Date:** _____

Directions: Set up your bridge. Place the apple (squirrel) on it. Mark the results.

My bridge...	Yes	No
is at least 18 inches (46 cm) long.		
has no middle support.		
can support the weight of an apple.		

1. Would you consider your bridge to be a success? Why or why not?

_____

_____

_____

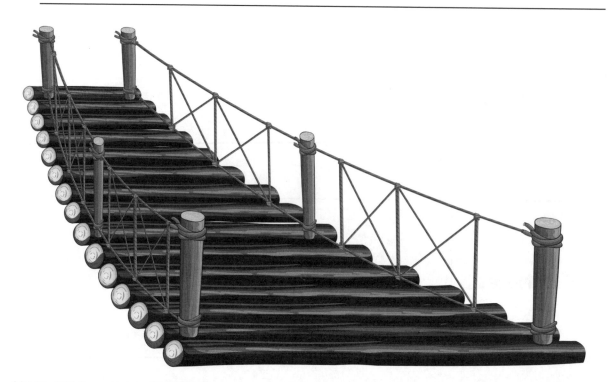

Name: _____ **Date:** _____

Directions: Think about your rope bridge design. Answer the questions. Then, plan how you want to improve it.

1. What went well with your bridge?

_____

_____

_____

2. What could make your bridge even better?

_____

_____

_____

Draw a star next to one or more ways you will improve your animal rope bridge.

- My design did not meet the criteria. I will improve it by

_____

- Make the bridge 24 inches (61 cm) across. It will reach over wider roads.
- Make the bridge stronger. Two squirrels (apples) will be able to cross safely.
- Make the bridge look more natural. It will blend into the surroundings.

Name: _____ **Date:** _____

Directions: Plan your new animal rope bridge design. Then, sketch your new design. Circle any parts or materials that are different or new. Then, complete the sentence.

In my redesign, I will…

add _____

remove _____

change _____

1. This design will work better because _____

_____

Name: _____ Date: _____

Directions: List and gather your materials. Plan your steps. Rebuild your rope bridge. Record notes as you build.

Materials

_____   _____

_____   _____

_____   _____

Steps to Rebuild My Animal Rope Bridge

_____

_____

_____

Building Notes

Problems	
Changes	
Other Notes	

 Quick Tip!

You do not have to start from scratch.
You can adjust your first bridge design.

Name: _____ Date: _____

Directions: Set up your bridge. Place the apple or apples on it. Complete the sentences in the table based on the goals you set. Mark the results.

My bridge...	Yes	No
is at least _____ long.		
has no middle support.		
can support the weight of _____ apple(s).		

1. Do you think this bridge works better than your first design? What is your evidence?

_____

_____

_____

Name: _____ Date: _____

Directions: Think about how you worked on this challenge. Answer the questions.

1. What are you most proud of about this challenge?

   _____

   _____

2. What would you do differently next time?

   _____

   _____

3. What did you learn from this challenge?

   _____

   _____

4. How would your bridge be different if it were built for actual use?

   _____

   _____

Talk About It!

What other animals might use your bridge? What animals in your area could benefit from an animal bridge?

Life Cycles of Plants Teaching Support

Overview of Unit Activities

Students will learn about and explore the life cycles of plants through the following activities:

- reading about life cycles of seed- and spore-producing plants
- reading about and studying pictures of how seeds are dispersed
- making simple greenhouses to grow bean plants
- making crayon rubbings of leaves, bark, and flowers
- analyzing a diagram of a tomato plant
- creating methods to make and explode seed pods

Materials Per Group

Week 1

- cotton balls (5)
- dry beans (pinto, lima, or kidney; 5)
- water
- zip-top bag

STEAM Challenge

- balloons (4–6; different size options if possible)
- basic school supplies
- birdseed ($\frac{1}{4}$ cup, 60 mL)
- butcher paper (*optional*; for seeds to disperse on)
- straw
- string (2–3 feet, 60–90 cm)
- thumbtacks or pushpins (2–3)
- zip-top baggies (2)

Setup and Instructional Tips

- **Week 1 Day 3:** Soak beans in water for one hour before students put them in baggies.
- **STEAM Challenge:** The challenge can be done individually or in groups. If students are working in groups, have students sketch their own designs first. Then, have them share designs in groups and choose one together.
- **Testing Days:** Remind students to be responsible and careful with thumbtacks. Tell students to leave space around balloons when/if they are popped.

Discussion Questions

- What does *life cycle* mean?
- Why are plants important?
- What do plants need to grow?
- Why is seed dispersal an important part of a plant's life cycle?

Additional Notes

- **Possible Design Solutions:** Students might choose to use balloons as their seed pods. Plastic bags might also be used. They might experiment with adding different amounts of seed or air to their pods. Depending on the materials used, paper funnels might be helpful to fill balloons with seeds.

Scaffolding and Extension Suggestions

- Support students by showing them how to make paper funnels and use them to pour seeds into balloons.
- Challenge students to create and test other methods of seed dispersal, such as seeds carried by wind or water.

Answer Key

Week 1 Day 1
1. B
2. A
3. D

Week 1 Day 2
1. Seeds need to go to different places so they do not have to compete for water, nutrients, and space.

Week 1 Day 5
1. Flowers are blooming.
2. About 2.5 months (or 70 days).
3. The tomatoes will be ready in late July or early August.

Weeks 2 & 3
See STEAM Challenge Rubric on page 221.

Name: _____ Date: _____

Directions: Read the text, and study the picture. Then, answer the questions.

The life cycle of a plant begins with a seed. A seed needs three things to begin growing: water, sunlight, and soil. When these needs are met, a seed will begin to sprout. This is called *germination*. The plant grows until it is mature, or fully grown. Depending on the type of plant, it might produce flowers, fruits, or vegetables.

Some plants do not grow from seeds. Plants such as moss and ferns grow from spores. Spores and seeds both grow into plants. Seeds are made of different kinds of cells. Spores only have one kind of cell.

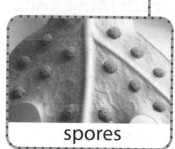

seed

spores

1. What is germination?

   (A) a plant producing flowers

   (B) a seed beginning to sprout

   (C) a plant growing from spores

   (D) a seed that is unable to grow

2. Which plant grows from a spore?

   (A) fern

   (B) daisy

   (C) tomato plant

   (D) apple tree

3. How are seeds and spores the same?

   (A) They both have different kinds of cells.

   (B) They both have one kind of cell.

   (C) They both grow moss.

   (D) They both grow into plants.

Name: _____ Date: _____

Directions: Read the text, and study the pictures. Then, answer the questions.

Seed dispersal is an important part of a plant's life cycle. Seeds need to spread to new places to grow. If they grow in the same spot, they will compete for water, nutrients, and space. There are many ways seeds move to new places.

Wind	Explosion	Animals	Water
	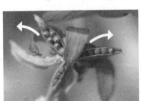		
A dandelion's seeds are very light. They are easily scattered by the wind.	Some plants, like the wild violet, have seed pods. The pods explode and scatter the seeds.	Acorns are an oak tree's seeds. Squirrels gather and bury them in different places.	A lotus flower's seeds are spongy. They float on the water and find new places to grow.

1. Why is seed dispersal important?

_____

_____

_____

_____

Day 3

Name: _____ **Date:** _____

Directions: Follow the steps to create a mini greenhouse. Grow a bean plant in your greenhouse.

A greenhouse is a building used for growing plants. It traps heat and moisture inside. This helps seeds germinate and grow into plants in cold places.

Materials

cotton balls	dry beans
water	zip-top bags

1. Soak beans in water for a few hours.

2. Dip cotton balls in water, and squeeze out excess water.

3. Put a few beans and cotton balls into a zip-top bag. Try to have each bean touch one cotton ball.

4. Seal the bag shut.

5. Tape the bag to a window, or make sure it is near sunlight.

6. Watch your bean sprout over the next few weeks! Share your observations with others.

Name: _____ **Date:** _____

Directions: Follow the steps to create rubbings of plant parts.

1. Go outside and gather leaves, flowers, bark, or other parts of plants. Be sure to look for items on the ground. Do not pick live plants.

2. Put the objects beneath a sheet of paper.

3. Use crayon or colored pencils to gently color over the plant parts. You can also try putting a crayon on its side and rubbing it.

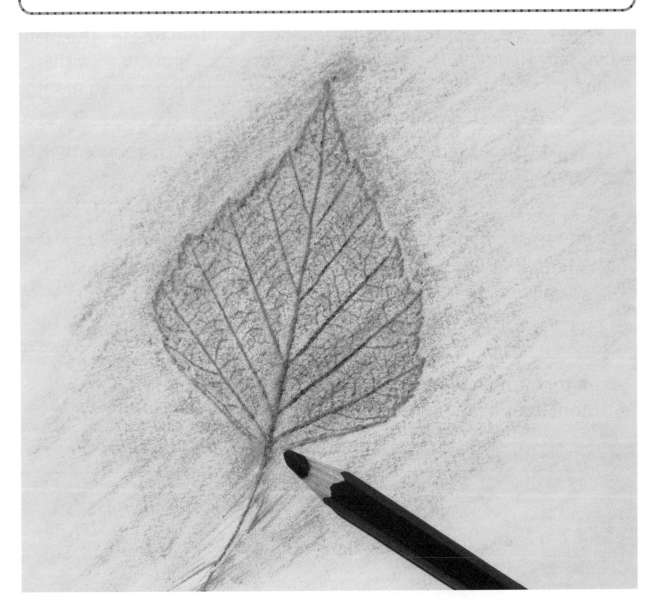

Name: _____ Date: _____

Directions: Study the diagram. Then, answer the questions.

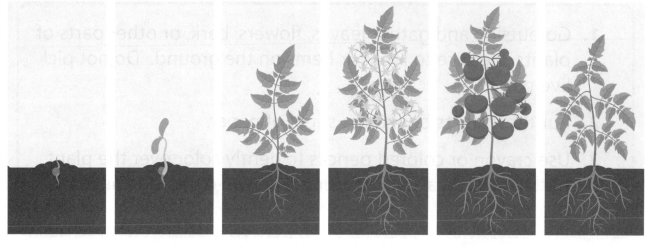

| The seeds are planted. (0 days) | The seeds sprout. (25 days) | The plant grows. (50 days) | Flowers bloom. (90 days) | Tomatoes grow. (110 days) | The plant withers. (6 months) |

1. What happens to the tomato plant after about three months of growth?

   _____

2. About how long will tomatoes grow before the plant begins to wilt?

   _____

3. If tomato seeds are planted in April, in what month will the tomatoes be ready?

   _____

Name: _____ Date: _____

Directions: Read the text. Then, answer the questions.

The Challenge

Plants disperse their seeds in many ways. The most exciting just might be explosion! For this challenge, you will create a method to make and explode a seed pod. The object is to scatter seeds as far as possible when the seed pod explodes. The person or group whose seeds scatter the greatest distance wins!

Criterion

To be successful, your seed pod explosion must scatter birdseed as far as possible.

Constraints

- You may only use the materials provided to you.
- The seed pod must be placed on the ground to explode (but it may be held in place by a person or object).

1. What questions do you have?

_____

_____

2. Write the challenge in your own words.

_____

_____

_____

Name: _____ Date: _____

Directions: Research two plants that use explosion dispersal. Record information about each plant. Then, brainstorm ideas with others.

Example 1

Name of Plant	Sketch of Plant	Seed Dispersal Facts

Example 2

Name of Plant	Sketch of Plant	Seed Dispersal Facts

Talk About It!

What ideas do you have for your design? What will the pod look like? How will the seeds get inside? What materials will work best? How will you make the seed pod pop or explode?

Name: _____ Date: _____

Directions: Sketch a design for your seed pod. Show where the seeds will be. Label all the materials. Then, sketch or write how the seed pod will explode.

Day 3

Seed Pod Design

Explosion Method

Day 4

Name: _____ **Date:** _____

Directions: List and gather your materials. Plan your steps for building your seed pod. Then, plan your method for making it explode. Build your seed pod. Record notes as you build.

Materials

_____   _____

_____   _____

_____   _____

Steps to Make and Explode My Seed Pod

_____

_____

_____

_____

Building Notes
(challenges, surprises, changes, etc.)

Day 5

Name: _____ Date: _____

Directions: Place your seed pod on the ground. Follow your plan to make your seed pod explode. Measure the distance from the pod to the farthest seed. Record the results. Then, draw a picture from a bird's-eye view of the seed dispersal.

Dispersal Distance

(in feet and inches) _____

(in meters and centimeters) _____

Day 1

Name: _____ Date: _____

Directions: Think about your seed pod and dispersal method. Answer the questions. Then, plan how you want to improve it.

1. What went well with your seed pod dispersal?

   _____

   _____

2. What could make your seed pod even better?

   _____

   _____

   The following constraint has been adjusted:

   • You may position your seed pod off the ground, but a person may not hold it.

3. How might you set up your seed pod so it is off the ground?

   _____

   _____

4. Do you think this will make your seeds travel farther? Why or why not?

   _____

   _____

Name: _____ Date: _____

Directions: Plan your new seed pod design. Then, sketch your new design. Then, sketch or write your new method for making your seed pod explode.

In my redesign, I will…

add _____

remove _____

change _____

New Seed Pod Design

New Explosion Method

Name: _____ Date: _____

Directions: List and gather your materials. Plan your steps for rebuilding your seed pod. Then, plan your new method for making it explode. Build your seed pod. Record notes as you build.

Materials

_____   _____

_____   _____

_____   _____

Steps to Make and Explode My Seed Pod

_____

_____

_____

_____

Building Notes
(challenges, surprises, changes, etc.)

Name: _____ **Date:** _____

Directions: Set up your seed pod. Follow your plan to make your seed pod explode. Measure the distance from the pod to the farthest seed. Record the results. Sketch a bird's-eye view of the seed dispersal. Then, answer the question.

> **Dispersal Distance**
>
> (in feet and inches) _____
>
> (in meters and centimeters) _____

1. Did your new seed pod and explosion method work better? What is your evidence?

_____

_____

Day 5

Name: _____ Date: _____

Directions: Compare your seed pod and explosion methods in the Venn diagram. Compare how they looked and worked. Then, answer the questions.

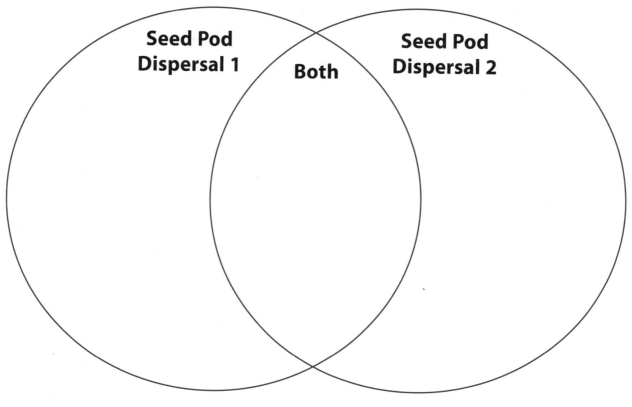

Seed Pod Dispersal 1

Both

Seed Pod Dispersal 2

1. What did you learn during this challenge?

   _____

   _____

2. Do you think explosion is an effective way to disperse seeds? Why or why not?

   _____

   _____

   _____

Fossils Teaching Support

Overview of Unit Activities

Students will learn about and explore fossils through the following activities:

- reading about what scientists can learn from fossils
- reading about and studying pictures of different types of fossils
- excavating toy fossils from plaster
- analyzing a flowchart showing how fossils form
- creating fossils and display cases

Materials Per Group

Week 1

- basic school supplies
- excavation tools (plastic knives, straws, paintbrushes, etc.)
- muffin tin or ice cube tray
- plaster of paris (from a craft store or homemade, using a ratio of 1:2 parts water to school glue)
- small toy or object

STEAM Challenge

- air-dry clay or modeling clay
- basic school supplies
- clothespins (4–5)
- craft sticks (10–15)
- objects to make fossils (leaves, shells, toys with feet for footprints, etc.)
- pipe cleaners (10–15)
- plastic wrap
- transparent film sheets or sheet protectors (4–6)
- wooden dowels (10–15)

Setup and Instructional Tips

- **Week 1 Day 3:** Homemade plaster of paris must be used within 15-20 minutes. It can take 30 minutes to an hour to be dry enough to remove from a mold. Leftover plaster of paris should be put into a trash can, not a sink.

- **STEAM Challenge:** The challenge can be done individually or in groups. If students are working in groups, have students sketch their own designs first. Then, have them share designs in groups and choose one together.

Discussion Questions

- What are fossils?
- How do fossils help us learn about the past?
- How are fossils made?
- Why is learning about the past important?

Additional Notes

- **Possible Misconception:** Fossils are buried deep in the ground.
  Truth: Because of erosion, some fossils may be close to the surface.
- **Possible Design Solutions:** Students might place their fossils between transparent sheets and add frames and support around them. Students might build box frames and cover the sides with transparent materials. They might make stands for their fossils or place them on ends of sticks.

Scaffolding and Extension Suggestions

- Take students on a virtual tour of a museum with many fossils on display, such as those provided by the National Museum of Natural History.
- Challenge students to create cast fossils to put in their display cases.

Answer Key

Week 1 Day 1
1. D
2. B
3. D

Week 1 Day 2
1. A scientist could learn about an animal's size, how it moved, or where it lived.
2. A mold fossil shows the imprint of something. A cast fossil is more like a 3D model.

Week 1 Day 5
1. The fish's bones became fossils.
2. The scientist learned that the land used to be the sea.

Weeks 2 & 3
See STEAM Challenge Rubric on page 221.

Name: _____ Date: _____

Directions: Read the text, and study the picture. Then, answer the questions.

Fossils are the remains of living things. Over time, parts of living things turn into stone. It takes millions of years. Shells, bones, and footprints can all become fossils. Sometimes, an entire skeleton can be a fossil. Or, a fossil might be a small leaf.

Fossils give clues about life long ago. Scientists can study fossils. This helps them learn about plants and animals. Many of them are extinct, or have no living members left. Their fossils are the only way to learn about them. Fossils can reveal how big a creature was, what it looked like, and where it lived. People who study fossils have a special name. They are paleontologists.

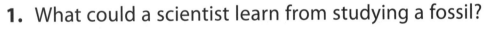

1. What could a scientist learn from studying a fossil?

Ⓐ how a plant went extinct

Ⓒ what a plant smelled like

Ⓑ the color of an animal

Ⓓ the size of an animal

2. Which item could *not* turn into a fossil?

Ⓐ bone

Ⓒ shell

Ⓑ rock

Ⓓ footprint

3. What does *extinct* mean?

Ⓐ an impression of a shell

Ⓒ searching for fossils

Ⓑ a plant from long ago

Ⓓ no living members are left

Name: _____ Date: _____

Directions: Read the text, and study the pictures. Then, answer the questions.

There are several types of fossils. This chart shows a few.

Mold	Trace	Cast

These fossils form when a plant, shell, or animal is pressed into the ground. A full imprint is made of its shape.	These fossils show evidence of activity. They are not of the animal but of a trace it leaves behind. It could be a footprint, a burrow, or droppings.	These fossils are made when a mold, or impression, is filled with material. Then, that material hardens. A 3D fossil of the original living thing is made.

1. What could a scientist learn about an animal from a trace fossil?

_____

_____

2. How are mold and cast fossils different?

_____

_____

Name: _____ **Date:** _____

Directions: Read the text. Follow the steps to make and excavate toy fossils.

> Fossils are often buried in the ground. Scientists must dig very carefully. This is called excavating. For this activity, you will excavate items dried in plaster of paris.

Materials

ice cube tray or muffin tin   paintbrush   plaster of paris

plastic knife and fork   small toys or objects

1. Pour a little plaster into the bottom of the tray or tin.

2. Add a small toy or object, and cover it with more plaster.

3. Let it dry for 30 to 60 minutes. Then, remove it from the tray or tin.

4. Trade "fossils" with a classmate.

5. Use tools to carefully excavate your item from the dried plaster.

Day 4

Name: _____ Date: _____

Directions: Look at the fossils found on an imaginary planet. One is of leaves, and one is of footprints. Choose one and draw what the living thing might have looked like. Use the fossil shape and size as clues.

Name: _____ Date: _____

Directions: Study the diagram. Then, answer the questions.

How a Fossil Forms

The fish dies and sinks to the bottom of the sea.

The fish decays, leaving its bones behind.

Over millions of years, the bones turn to rock and become fossils.

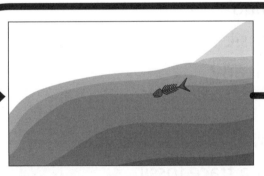 

Over time, the sea dries up and becomes land.

A scientist finds the fossil and learns the land used to be covered in water.

1. What parts of the fish became fossils?

_____

2. What did the scientist learn from the fossil?

_____

_____

Name: _____ Date: _____

Directions: Read the text. Then, answer the questions.

The Challenge

Many people find fossils fascinating. They like to look for them in nature. A palentologist's job is to find fossils. When they find one, they treat it carefully. They clean it and try to figure out what made it. Many fossils are on display in museums. For this challenge, you will make a fossil. Then, you will create a display case for the fossil.

Criteria

To be successful, your fossil case must…

- display a fossil of a living thing.
- provide protection to the fossil.
- allow the fossil to be seen clearly.

Constraints

- You may only use the materials provided to you.
- The fossil must be a mold or a trace fossil.

1. What questions do you have?

_____

_____

2. What are you looking forward to?

_____

_____

Day 2

Name: _____ **Date:** _____

Directions: Research fossil display cases. Answer the questions based on your findings.

1. What type of fossil will you make?

mold   trace

2. What could your fossil be of? Write all the ideas you have.

_____

_____

3. Draw two examples of fossil display cases. Show their shapes and how the fossils are positioned or supported.

4. What ideas do you like in the examples you found?

_____

_____

_____

Name: _____ **Date:** _____

Directions: Sketch a design for your fossil display case. Show your fossil in the case. Show how it will be positioned or supported. Label the materials. Then, complete the sentences.

This design protects the fossil because _____

_____

This design allows the fossil to be seen clearly and easily because

_____

Name: _____ **Date:** _____

Directions: Make your mold or trace fossil. While it dries, list and gather your materials for your display case. Plan your steps. Build your display case.

> To make your fossil…
>
> 1. Shape your clay however you want it. It might be flat, round, or irregular. Place it on wax paper.
>
> 2. Press the object of your choice into the clay so it leaves an imprint.
>
> 3. Let the clay dry.

Materials

_____   _____

_____   _____

_____   _____

Steps to Build My Fossil Display Case

_____

_____

_____

_____

Day 5

Name: _____ Date: _____

Directions: Place your fossil in your display case. Answer questions about your design. Share it with others. Tell them about it. Show them how it meets the criteria. Ask them some questions. Write what they say.

Tell

1. How does your display case protect the fossil?

_____

2. How does your display case make the fossil easy to see?

_____

Show

Place your display case on a desk. Ask others to come look and observe the fossil without touching it.

Ask

3. What do you like about my display case?

_____

_____

4. How can I make it better?

_____

_____

5. What living thing do you think made this fossil?

_____

Name: _____ Date: _____

Directions: Think about your display case design. Answer the questions. Then, plan how you want to improve it.

1. Did your fossil and display case turn out as you expected? Why or why not?

   _____

   _____

2. Were people able to correctly guess what your fossil was?

   yes   no

   If not, was the display case or the fossil the problem?

   _____

3. What parts of your display case worked well?

   _____

   _____

   Draw a star next to one or more ways you will improve your design.

   - My design did not meet the criteria. I will improve it by

     _____

   - Make the fossil viewable from all angles.
   - Make the display case big enough to fit two fossils.

   - My own idea: _____

     _____

Day 2

Name: _____ **Date:** _____

Directions: Plan your new fossil display case design. Then, sketch your new design. Show your fossil in the case. Show how it will be positioned or supported. If you are adding a second fossil, draw that one also.

In my redesign, I will…

add _____

remove _____

change _____

Name: _____ Date: _____

Directions: Make a second fossil if that was part of your plan. Then, list and gather your materials for your new display case. Plan your steps. Rebuild your display case. Record notes as you build.

Materials

_____   _____

_____   _____

_____   _____

Steps to Build My Fossil Display Case

_____

_____

_____

Talk About It!

Did your new design turn out how you planned? Why or why not?

Name: _____ Date: _____

Directions: Place your fossil(s) in your display case. Answer questions about your new design. Share it with others. Tell them about it. Show them how it meets the criteria. Ask them some questions. Write what they say.

Tell

1. What improvements did you make?

_____

2. Why is your new display case design better?

_____

Show

Place your display case on a desk. Ask others to come look and observe the fossil(s) without touching it.

Ask

3. What do you like about my new display case?

_____

_____

4. How can I make it better?

_____

_____

5. What living thing do you think made this fossil?

_____

Day 5

Name: _____ **Date:** _____

Directions: Make your classroom into a fossil museum. Set your fossil display case in a place where others can see it. They should do the same with their fossil cases. Walk quietly around the room and observe all the fossils. Choose four to draw. Show the display case and the fossil for each.

Pollution Problems Teaching Support

Overview of Unit Activities

Students will learn about and explore causes and effects of pollution through the following activities:

- reading about different types of pollution
- reading about the effects of pollution
- cleaning up an oil spill simulation
- drawing before and after pollution pictures
- analyzing a graph about air quality
- creating storm drain covers

Materials Per Group

Week 1

- cotton balls (5–10)
- dish soap (a few drops)
- food coloring
- plastic spoon
- tin tray
- vegetable oil ($\frac{1}{4}$ cup, 60 mL)
- water

STEAM Challenge

- basic school supplies
- craft sticks (10–20)
- fabric (such as burlap or mesh)
- large bucket (to fill with water and trash)
- large plastic tub (to represent a drain)
- paper clips (20+)
- pipe cleaners (10–20)
- plastic wrap
- straws (10–20)
- trash items (cans, plastic bags, bottles, paper, etc.)
- water
- wood or metal dowels (10–20)

Setup and Instructional Tips

- **STEAM Challenge:** The challenge can be done individually or in groups. If students are working in groups, have students sketch their own designs first. Then, have them share designs in groups and choose one together.

- **Testing Days:** You (or students) will need to make "dirty water." This can be done by filling the bucket with water and pieces of trash.

Discussion Questions

- What is pollution?
- How is pollution harmful?
- How can people help the pollution problems on Earth?
- What is a watershed?
- Why are storm drains needed?
- What problems can be caused by storm drains?

Additional Notes

- **Possible Misconception:** Pollution is permanent.
  Truth: There are many ways to reduce current pollution levels by using renewable energy, recycling, and building back forests.
- **Possible Design Solutions:** Students might construct grid coverings with open holes. They might also use something with a tight weave, such as fabric. Students might lay their covers on the plastic tub, or they might use something to hold it in place.

Scaffolding and Extension Suggestions

- Walk around your school or neighborhood, and have students look for storm drains.
- Encourage students to write to government officials about reducing pollution.

Answer Key

Week 1 Day 1
1. D
2. A
3. C

Week 1 Day 2
1. Runoff is when trash on the land gets into the water and makes water pollution.
2. Rain can carry pollution to rivers that then lead to oceans.

Week 1 Day 5
1. The air quality is getting worse.
2. *Example:* A fire with lots of smoke is happening.

Weeks 2 & 3
See STEAM Challenge Rubric on page 221.

Day 1

Name: _____ Date: _____

Directions: Read the text. Then, answer the questions.

Pollution makes the environment dirty. There are three main types. They are land, water, and air pollution.

When people litter, they pollute the land. Also, some farmers use chemicals. This keeps bugs away from their crops. But the chemicals can seep into the ground. Sometimes, trash ends up in oceans and rivers. Oil companies have spilled oil into the ocean. Factories and cars burn fossil fuels. This can release small particles and gas into the air.

Pollution affects people, animals, and plants. Polluted air can make it harder to breathe. Drinking dirty water causes illness. Litter can make towns and cities look dirty. Pollution is dangerous.

1. How can farmers cause pollution?

   Ⓐ The crops they grow have bugs.

   Ⓑ Their equipment is large and expensive.

   Ⓒ They burn fossil fuels.

   Ⓓ The chemicals they use go into the ground.

2. _____ can burn fossil fuels.

   Ⓐ Cars

   Ⓑ Litter

   Ⓒ Animal habitats

   Ⓓ Chemicals

3. Which pollution is an example of land pollution?

   Ⓐ oil spills

   Ⓑ fossil fuels

   Ⓒ litter

   Ⓓ gas

Name: _____   Date: _____

Directions: Read the text, and study the diagram. Then, answer the questions.

Runoff is when things in or on the land are carried away by water. Runoff causes pollution problems. Land pollution can become water pollution. Chemicals can be in the ground. They can get washed into a creek when it rains. Wind can blow litter in a park. It might blow it into a storm drain. Creeks and storm drains empty into larger bodies of water. The pollution spreads.

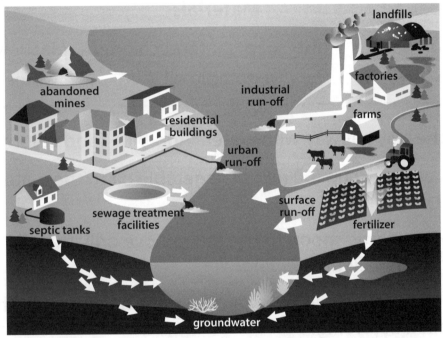

1. Define *runoff* in your own words.

_____

_____

2. How can weather affect pollution?

_____

_____

Name: _____ Date: _____

Directions: Read the text. Follow the steps to try different methods for cleaning up an oil spill.

> Oil is used to power factories and cars. It is shipped across the ocean. Sometimes, there are accidents. Millions of gallons of oil can spill into the water. This causes big problems! There are three methods for cleaning up the mess. Give them a try.

Materials

cotton balls	dish soap	food coloring	plastic spoons
tin tray	vegetable oil		water

1. Fill the tray halfway with water. Add blue food coloring and stir.

2. Add about $\frac{1}{4}$ cup (60 mL) of vegetable oil to the water. This is your oil spill.

3. Use the plastic spoon to try and remove only the oil. This method is called *skimming*.

4. Use the cotton balls to try and remove only the oil. This method is called *absorbing*.

5. Add a few drops of dish soap to the water and stir. This method is called *dispersing*.

 Talk About It!

Which method do you think worked best?
How could oil spills affect animals?

Name: _____ Date: _____

Directions: Choose a place, such as a forest, a city, or your neighborhood. Draw a before and after picture of the place. The before picture should show pollution. The after picture should show the place after people have cleaned it up and stopped polluting.

Before

After

Name: _____ Date: _____

Directions: Read the text, and study the graph. Then, answer the questions.

> Scientists assign a number to the air quality. If the air is clean and healthy, it will have a low score. The higher the number, the worse the air quality.
>
> | Good | Moderate | Unhealthy for Sensitive Groups | Unhealthy | Very Unhealthy | Hazardous |
> |------|----------|-------------------------------|-----------|----------------|-----------|

Sunday	Monday	Tuesday	Wednesday	Thursday	Friday	Saturday
Good	Good	Moderate	Moderate	Unhealthy for Sensitive Groups	Unhealthy for Sensitive Groups	Unhealthy

1. The predicted air quality for the week is shown in the table. What pattern do you see over the week?

_____

_____

2. What might be causing the change?

_____

_____

Name: _____ Date: _____

Directions: Read the text. Then, answer the questions.

The Challenge

Rain can cause flooding in streets. For safety reasons, there are gutters with drains along the sides of roads. They help drain the water. Litter often ends up down in the gutters, too. This makes extra work when the water is filtered. Sometimes, the water drains right into the ocean. For this challenge, you will create a cover for a storm drain to keep out trash.

Criteria

To be successful, your storm drain cover must…

- filter out as much litter as possible.
- allow water to flow freely through it.

Constraints

- You may only use the materials provided to you.
- Your cover must fit over the "drain" (plastic tub).

1. What are you wondering?

_____

_____

2. Write the challenge in your own words.

_____

_____

Day 2

Name: _____ Date: _____

Directions: Research storm drains. Draw two examples of covers that help keep out trash. Then, answer the questions.

Storm Drain Example 1	Storm Drain Example 2

1. How are the examples similar? How are they different?

   _____

   _____

2. What other ideas do you have to block trash but let water flow through? Draw or write all your ideas.

Name: _____ **Date:** _____

Directions: Sketch two designs for your storm drain cover. Try to make them very different. Draw a star next to the one you think will work best. List the materials.

Design 1

Design 2

Materials

_____   _____

_____   _____

_____

Name: _____ **Date:** _____

Directions: Gather your materials. Answer the questions. Plan your steps. Build your storm drain cover. Record notes as you build.

1. What concerns do you have about your gutter cover?

   _____

   _____

2. Write a prediction about how your cover will perform.

   _____

   _____

Steps to Build My Storm Drain Cover

_____

_____

_____

My Building Notes	
Challenges	
Changes	
Other Notes	

Day 5

Name: _____ **Date:** _____

Directions: Fill a bucket with water and pieces of trash. Place your storm drain cover over a plastic tub. Pour the bucket of water over the storm drain cover into the plastic tub. Record your results.

1. How many pieces of trash were in your bucket? _____

2. How many pieces of trash were caught by the filter? _____

3. Did your cover slow down the water flow? Explain how you know.

   _____

   _____

4. Draw your storm drain after pouring the dirty water over it.

Name: _____ **Date:** _____

Directions: Think about your storm drain cover design. Answer the questions. Then, plan how you want to improve it.

1. What went well with your storm drain cover?

   _____

   _____

2. What could make your cover work even better?

   _____

   _____

> The following testing constraints have been adjusted.
>
> - At least 15 pieces of trash must be in the dirty water.
> - All pieces of trash must be smaller than a 6-inch (15 cm) square.

3. How will these new constraints affect your design? What changes will you need to make?

   _____

   _____

   _____

   _____

Day 2

Name: _____ **Date:** _____

Directions: Plan your new storm drain cover design. Sketch your new design. Label the materials. Then, complete the sentence.

In my redesign, I will…

add _____

remove _____

change _____

1. This design will work better because _____

_____

Name: _____ Date: _____

Directions: Gather your materials. Answer the questions. Plan your steps. Rebuild your storm drain cover. Record notes as you build.

1. What concerns do you have about your new storm drain cover?

   _____

   _____

2. Write a prediction about how your new design will perform.

   _____

   _____

Steps to Rebuild My Storm Drain Cover

_____

_____

_____

My Building Notes	
Challenges	
Changes	
Other Notes	

Name: _____ Date: _____

Directions: Fill a bucket with water and smaller pieces of trash. Place your new storm drain cover over a plastic tub. Pour water over the storm drain cover into the plastic tub. Record your results.

1. How many pieces of trash were in your bucket? _____

2. How many pieces of trash were caught by the filter? _____

3. Did your cover slow down the water flow? Explain how you know.

   _____

   _____

4. Did this design work better? Explain your evidence.

   _____

   _____

5. Draw your storm drain after pouring the dirty water over it.

Unit 10: Pollution Problems

Name: _____ Date: _____

Directions: Think about how you worked on this challenge. Answer the questions.

1. Why is it important to filter trash from the water that goes into the drains?

   _____

   _____

2. Do you think your cover would work in real life? Why or why not?

   _____

   _____

3. Draw yourself doing something you enjoyed. Write a caption.	4. Draw yourself testing your design. Write a caption.

Severe Weather Hazards Teaching Support

Overview of Unit Activities

Students will learn about and explore types of severe weather hazards and ways to prepare for them through the following activities:

- reading about different types of severe weather
- reading about and studying pictures of floods
- making model landslides
- creating signs and symbols for different types of severe weather
- analyzing a map of tornado locations
- creating flood barriers

Materials Per Group

Week 1

- dirt or soil ($\frac{1}{2}$ cup, 125 mL)
- sand ($\frac{1}{2}$ cup, 125 mL)
- small chute (made of wood, plastic, cardboard, etc.)
- small objects to represent houses
- tin tray
- water

STEAM Challenge

- basic school supplies
- colander
- cotton balls (20–30)
- fabric
- foam pieces
- modeling clay
- paper towels (10–20 sheets)
- pitcher of water
- plastic tub
- ruler
- sand and/or dirt (2 cups, 500 mL)
- sponges or sponge pieces
- zip-top baggies (5–10)

Setup and Instructional Tips

- **STEAM Challenge:** The challenge can be done individually or in groups. If students are working in groups, have students sketch their own designs first. Then, have them share designs in groups and choose one together.

- **Building Days:** If students use sand or dirt in their barriers, make sure they put it in some sort of bag.

- **Testing Days:** During Week 2, students might place their houses at one end of the tub and pour water through the colander at the other end. The colander should soften the fall of water and mimic rain. During Week 3, students will pour water directly into the tub, but they should do it slowly. Templates for paper houses can be found online. Otherwise, students can crumble sheets of paper to represent houses.

Discussion Questions

- What are examples of severe weather?
- What can happen during severe weather?
- Does climate change affect severe weather? How?
- How does severe weather impact people's lives in different parts of the world?

Additional Notes

- **Possible Misconception:** Flooding only happens after heavy rain.
  Truth: Flooding can also be caused by snowmelt and changes in water routes.
- **Possible Design Solutions:** Students may put sand and dirt in baggies. They may layer various materials around their paper homes.

Scaffolding and Extension Suggestions

- Encourage students to research and find out which types of severe weather have impacted their communities or states.

Answer Key

Week 1 Day 1
1. B
2. D
3. B

Week 1 Day 2
1. You might prepare for a blizzard by getting food and firewood so you don't have to leave the house.
2. The rocks and soil could come down the hill and ruin homes and buildings.

Week 1 Day 5
1. Texas
2. They are mostly in the Midwest and central areas of the United States.
3. They might have tornado drills at school. They might talk with their families about where to go and what to do if there is a tornado.

Weeks 2 & 3
See STEAM Challenge Rubric on page 221.

Name: _____ Date: _____

Directions: Read the text, and study the picture. Then, answer the questions.

Day 1

There are many different types of severe weather. Floods, tornadoes, and blizzards are examples. So are hurricanes and tropical storms. They may not make the same weather, but they do have one thing in common. They can all be dangerous.

People cannot stop severe weather. There are things they can do to prepare for it, though.

Keep an eye on the weather. Watch the news or look online to see predictions.

Have a plan. Know a safe place to go in your home. It might be a basement, cellar, or bathroom.

Be prepared. Trim dead or loose branches off trees. People can board their windows and bring items from their porches or yards inside.

1. What do all types of severe weather have in common?

   (A) They bring rain.   (C) They have high winds.

   (B) They can be dangerous.   (D) They can be stopped.

2. Which place would be the safest if there were a tornado warning?

   (A) bedroom   (C) porch

   (B) kitchen   (D) basement

3. Why do you think loose tree branches should be trimmed?

   (A) They might get struck by lightning.   (C) They might be homes for birds.

   (B) They might fall on a house.   (D) They might grow too big.

Name: _____ Date: _____

Directions: Read the text. Then, answer the questions.

blizzard—a severe snowstorm that lasts for several hours

tornado—a violent windstorm on land in the shape of a funnel

flood—a large amount of water covering land that is usually dry

Types of Severe Weather and Weather Hazards

landslide—when rocks or soil quickly move down a hill or mountain

hurricane—a violent storm with wind and rain that begins in the ocean

storm surge—a rise in the seawater level caused by the winds of a storm

1. How might you prepare for a blizzard?

_____

_____

_____

2. How could people be affected by landslides?

_____

_____

Name: _____ Date: _____

Directions: Read the text. Follow the steps to create a model landslide.

A landslide can happen in hilly areas or by mountains. Heavy rains can cause the land to slide down. Earthquakes can also cause them.

Materials

sand   soil   tin tray   water

small chute   small objects to
(sloping surface with sides)   represent houses

1. Place the "houses" at one end of the tray. Place the chute on the other side. Tape the chute in place if needed.

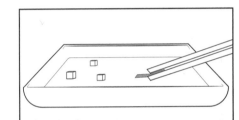

2. Put a small mound of soil halfway up the chute.

3. Fill a paper cup halfway with water. Slowly pour water down the chute, starting at the top.

4. Put a small mound of sand halfway up the chute.

5. Fill a paper cup halfway with water. Slowly pour water down the chute, starting at the top.

 Talk About It!

What happened to the soil? What happened to the sand? What happened to the houses?

Name: _____ Date: _____

Directions: Make some severe weather warning signs. Choose four types of severe weather. Draw a symbol or logo to represent a warning for each one.

Name: _____ **Date:** _____

Directions: Study the map. Then, answer the questions.

Average Number of Tornadoes Per Year (Top 10 States)

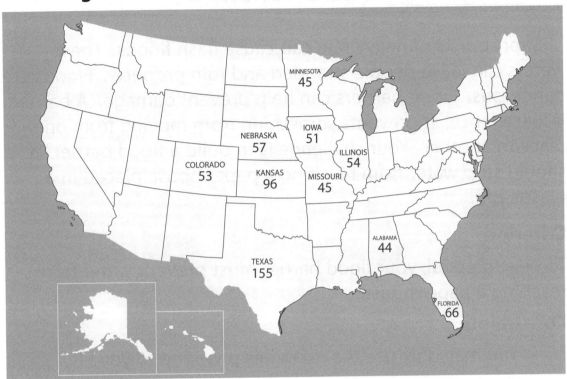

1. Which state has the most tornadoes per year?

   _____

2. What do you notice about the location of these states?

   _____

   _____

3. How might students prepare for tornadoes in these states?

   _____

   _____

Name: _____ Date: _____

Directions: Read the text. Then, answer the questions.

The Challenge

Short bursts of heavy rain can cause flash floods. These waters can leave people stranded and ruin property. Floods are dangerous. Flood barriers can help prevent damage. A barrier is like a fence. It prevents something from moving from one place to another. Your challenge is to build a flood barrier. It should stop water from reaching a paper house placed in a plastic tub.

Criterion

To be successful, your flood barrier must prevent water from reaching a paper house.

Constraints

- You may only use the materials provided to you.
- The barrier must not touch the paper house.

1. What is a barrier?

_____

_____

2. What questions do you have?

_____

_____

Name: _____ Date: _____

Directions: Research flooding and flood barriers. Answer the questions. Then, discuss your answers and ideas with others.

1. What causes floods?

_____

_____

2. Which types of places are more likely to flood?

_____

_____

3. What materials are used for real flood barriers?

_____

_____

4. What materials would be good for your flood barrier?

_____

_____

5. What other ideas do you have for your flood barrier? Draw or write as many as you can.

Name: _____ Date: _____

Directions: Sketch a design for your flood barrier. Label all the materials you plan to use.

sides of plastic tub

paper house

Think About It!

How tall should the barrier be? How thick should it be? How much space will there be between the barrier and the house?

Name: _____ Date: _____

Directions: Gather your materials. Plan your steps. Build your flood barrier. Record notes as you build.

> To make your paper house, choose one of the following options.
>
> - Loosely crumple a sheet of paper into a large ball. Tape it to the middle of the plastic tub.
> - Find directions online to make a more realistic looking paper house.

Steps to Build My Flood Barrier

_____

_____

_____

Building Notes
(challenges, surprises, discoveries, changes, etc.)

Name: _____ Date: _____

Directions: Pour several cups of water through the colander and into the tub. Use a ruler to measure the depth of water inside and outside the barrier. Record the results.

1. Depth of water outside the barrier.

   _____ inches   _____ centimeters

2. Depth of water inside the barrier.

   _____ inches   _____ centimeters

3. Draw how the house looks after the test.

   [ ]

4. Was your flood barrier successful? How do you know?

   _____

   _____

Day 1

Name: _____ Date: _____

Directions: Think about your flood barrier design. Answer the questions. Then, plan how you want to improve it.

1. Which materials do you think worked best to block water?

_____

_____

2. What issues or problems do you need to fix to make your design work better?

_____

_____

> Did your first flood barrier keep the house dry? If so, it is time to increase the difficulty of the challenge. When you test your new design, add twice as much water. Add the water directly into the tub. Do not use a colander.

3. What changes could you make to your flood barrier to make it block more water? Write or draw all your ideas.

┌─────────────────────────────────────┐
│   │
│   │
│   │
│   │
│   │
└─────────────────────────────────────┘

Day 2

Name: _____ **Date:** _____

Directions: Plan your new flood barrier design. Then, sketch your design. Label all materials you plan to use.

In my redesign, I will…

add _____

remove _____

change _____

sides of plastic tub

paper house

Name: _____ Date: _____

Directions: Dry your tub. Make a new paper house, and tape it to the center of the tub. Gather your materials. Plan your steps. Rebuild your flood barrier. Record notes as you build.

Think About It!

What new materials do you need? How do you need to change your steps?

Steps to Rebuild My Flood Barrier

_____

_____

_____

Building Notes
(challenges, surprises, discoveries, changes, etc.)

Day 4

Name: _____ Date: _____

Directions: Pour several cups of water into the tub. If your first design worked, double the amount of water. Use a ruler to measure the depth of water inside and outside the barrier. Then, answer the questions.

1. Depth of water outside the barrier.

   _____ inches   _____ centimeters

2. Depth of water inside the barrier.

   _____ inches   _____ centimeters

3. Draw how the house looks after the test.

4. Did your new flood barrier design work better? How do you know?

   _____

   _____

Name: _____ **Date:** _____

Directions: Think about how you worked on this challenge. Answer the questions.

1. What was difficult about this challenge?

_____

_____

2. What do you think would be challenging about creating barriers in real life?

_____

_____

3. Draw yourself building your storm barrier. Write a caption.	**4.** Draw yourself testing your design. Write a caption.

 Talk About It!

What other ways do you think engineers help prevent severe weather hazards?

Measuring the Weather Teaching Support

Overview of Unit Activities

Students will learn about and explore weather instruments and forecasts through the following activities:

- reading about and studying pictures of barometers
- reading about and studying pictures of various weather instruments
- making weather vanes to track the weather
- drawing weather scenes
- analyzing a weekly weather forecast
- creating interactive classroom weather station charts

Materials Per Group

Week 1

- basic school supplies
- paper cup
- pushpins
- straw
- sturdy paper plate

STEAM Challenge

- basic school supplies
- brads (3–4)
- construction paper
- hook and loop pieces (optional)
- paper clips (10+)
- paper plates (2–3)
- pipe cleaners (5–10)
- poster board
- string (2–3 feet, 60–90 cm)

Setup and Instructional Tips

- **STEAM Challenge:** The challenge can be done individually or in groups. If students are working in groups, have students sketch their own designs first. Then, have them share designs in groups and choose one together.

Discussion Questions

- Why would someone want to know a weather forecast for tomorrow?
- How do you think people predict the weather?
- What types of tools do people use to learn about weather?
- How does weather impact your daily life?

Additional Notes

- **Possible Design Solutions:** Students may create weather wheels to put on their charts to mark sky conditions each day. They may create thermometers and barometers with moving arrows. They might create pieces that can be attached and removed to show types of weather each day.

Scaffolding and Extension Suggestions

- Tour different classrooms to see what weather information they monitor each day.
- Encourage students to keep a weather journal for a month and record the temperature, precipitation, and the rising and falling of barometric pressure.

Answer Key

Week 1 Day 1
1. D
2. A
3. B

Week 1 Day 2
1. thermometer
2. Answer should state which instrument students think would be the easiest to use and tell why.

Week 1 Day 5
1. Wednesday
2. The air pressure is falling because it is getting cooler, cloudier, and it rains on Wednesday.
3. Answer should tell which day's weather students like the most and why.

Weeks 2 & 3
See STEAM Challenge Rubric on page 221.

Name: _____ Date: _____

Directions: Read the text, and study the picture. Then, answer the questions.

Weather forecasts help people make plans and know what to expect. But how are forecasts made? A barometer is one tool used. It looks a little like a clock. But it does not measure time. It measures the pressure of the air. Earth's atmosphere has weight. This means gravity pulls it toward Earth. The air presses on everything as it is pulled down.

barometer

Air pressure can fall. This means it gets lower, and there isn't enough pressure to push away storm clouds. Low pressure often brings rain and bad weather. Air pressure can also rise. This means it gets higher. There is enough pressure to push away clouds. Rising pressure means clear and dry days.

1. What does a barometer do?

    Ⓐ measures temperature   Ⓒ measures gravity

    Ⓑ measures time   Ⓓ measures air pressure

2. Rising air pressure brings what kind of weather?

    Ⓐ clear   Ⓑ rainy   Ⓒ stormy   Ⓓ hot

3. Why does gravity pull on the atmosphere?

    Ⓐ The atmosphere has pressure.   Ⓒ Gravity measures the pressure.

    Ⓑ The atmosphere has weight.   Ⓓ Gravity has weight.

Name: _____ **Date:** _____

Directions: Read the text, and study the pictures. Then, answer the questions.

People who study weather are called meteorologists. They use many tools. Here are some instruments they use.

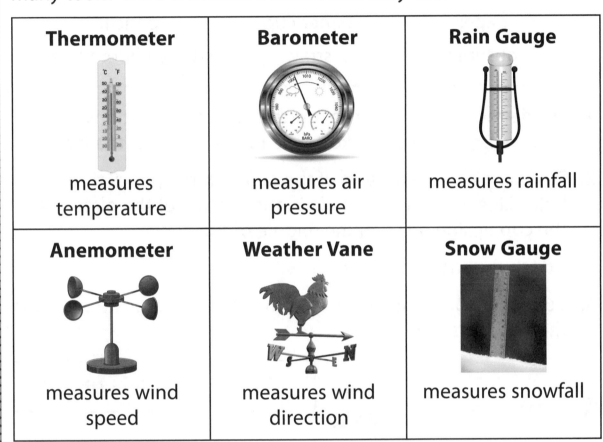

Thermometer	Barometer	Rain Gauge
measures temperature	measures air pressure	measures rainfall
Anemometer	Weather Vane	Snow Gauge
measures wind speed	measures wind direction	measures snowfall

1. Which instrument would let you know if you should wear a warm jacket?

   _____

2. Which do you think would be the simplest to use? Why?

   _____

   _____

Day 3

Name: _____ Date: _____

Directions: Follow the directions to build a weather vane. Then, use the weather vane to check the direction of the wind for three days. Record the directions in the table.

> **Materials**
>
> | paper | paper cup | pencil |
> | pushpin | straw | sturdy paper plate |

1. Divide the paper plate into fourths. Label the sections *north*, *south*, *east*, and *west*. Poke a hole in the center of the plate.

2. Poke a hole in the bottom of the cup. Put the pencil through the hole. Line it up with the hole in the bottom of the plate. Glue the cup upside down in the middle of the plate.

3. Attach the straw to the pencil with a pushpin.

4. Cut out shapes that look like the tip and end of an arrow. Tape them to the straw.

Date	Wind Direction

Name: _____ Date: _____

Directions: As the seasons change, so does a landscape. Draw a nature scene for each of the four seasons. Add a character to the frames. Draw your character in each scene. Show what they do and wear.

Day 4

Spring	Summer
Fall	**Winter**

Try This!

Use a brad to attach a paper arrow to the center of the seasons. Move the arrow to show what season it is.

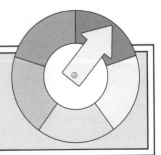

Name: _____ **Date:** _____

Directions: Study the weather forecast. Then, answer the questions.

Sunday	Monday	Tuesday	Wednesday	Thursday	Friday	Saturday
☀️	🌤️	☁️	🌧️	☁️	🌤️	☀️
72 oF	66 oF	60 oF	55 oF	67 oF	72 oF	76 oF

1. A baseball game was canceled due to weather. What day was the game most likely on?

   _____

2. What do you think is happening to the air pressure from Sunday to Wednesday? Why?

   _____

   _____

3. Which day's weather do you like the most? Why?

   _____

   _____

Name: _____ Date: _____

Directions: Read the text. Then, answer the questions.

The Challenge

A class at your school wants to observe and record the weather every day. The teacher has asked for your help. They have asked you to make a weather recording chart. The teacher wants it to be interactive and fun. They want it to have parts that students can move and change to show the weather.

Criteria

To be successful, your weather chart must…

- have places to show three or more daily weather observations or measurements.
- be interactive in some way (moving parts or pieces).

Constraints

- You may only use the materials provided to you.
- Your design must fit on a standard-size poster board (22" x 28").

1. What have you been asked to make?

_____

_____

2. Who are you making it for? How might that guide your design?

_____

_____

Name: _____ **Date:** _____

Directions: Research examples of weather charts online. Think of weather charts you have used before. Visit other classrooms to see what they have. Record ideas in the boxes. Add your own ideas. Share them with others. Then, answer the question.

Weather Measurements or Observations	Parts That Move or Change (ex: arrows on weather wheel)
Pictures or Designs	**Unique or Fun Ideas**

1. What types of weather information will you include in your chart? Circle at least three.

air pressure   wind speed

temperature

cloud conditions   wind direction

Name: _____ **Date:** _____

Directions: Sketch a design for your weather chart. Show how the parts can move or change. List the materials.

Materials

_____   _____

_____   _____

_____   _____

Name: _____ **Date:** _____

Directions: Gather your materials. Your weather chart will have different parts. Plan what each person in your group will do. Make your weather chart. Record notes as you build.

Weather Chart Group Plan

	Job or Section of Chart	Group Member(s)
1		
2		
3		
4		
5		
6		

Building Notes
(challenges, surprises, discoveries, changes, etc.)

Name: _____ **Date:** _____

Directions: Assess your weather chart. Mark the criteria that it meets. Write notes to explain or describe the results. Then, share your weather chart with others. Ask them some questions. Record their answers.

Criteria	✓	Notes
My weather chart has three or more weather measurements or observations.		
My weather chart has interactive parts. (Parts can move or change to show the weather.)		
My weather chart has fun and neat designs.		

Feedback

1. What do you like best about my weather chart?

_____

_____

2. How could I make it better?

_____

_____

Name: _____ Date: _____

Directions: Think about your weather chart design. Answer the questions. Then, plan how you want to improve it.

1. What parts of your weather chart do you think work well?

   _____

   _____

   _____

2. What changes do you think you need to make?

   _____

   _____

   _____

   Draw a star next to one or more ways you will improve your weather chart.

   - My design did not meet the criteria. I will improve it by

     _____

     _____

   - Add a weather forecast section to your chart.

   - My own idea: _____

     _____

Day 2

Name: _____ **Date:** _____

Directions: Plan your new weather chart design. Then, sketch your new design. Label the parts and materials.

In my redesign, I will…

add _____

remove _____

change _____

Name: _____ Date: _____

Directions: Gather your materials. Plan what each person in your group will do. Rebuild your weather chart. Record notes as you build.

💡 **Quick Tip!**

You do not need to start from scratch. You can make changes to your first weather chart design. Think about how that will change the jobs that need to be done.

Weather Chart Group Plan

	Job or Section of Chart	Group Member(s)
1		
2		
3		
4		
5		
6		

Building Notes
(challenges, surprises, discoveries, changes, etc.)

Day 4

Name: _____ **Date:** _____

Directions: Write any new goals you set in the table. Assess your new weather chart design. Mark the criteria that it meets. Write notes to explain or describe the results. Share your new weather chart with others. Then, answer the question.

Criteria	✓	Notes
My weather chart has three or more weather measurements or observations.		
My weather chart has interactive parts. (Parts can move or change to show the weather.)		
My weather chart has fun and neat designs.		

1. Is your new weather chart better? Why do you think so?

_____

_____

Name: _____ Date: _____

Directions: Think about how you worked on this challenge. Answer the questions.

1. What are you most proud of about this challenge?

   _____

   _____

2. Draw your weather chart in use in a classroom. Write a caption to tell what is happening.

Try This!

Use your weather chart at home or school for a week or more. Make a weather forecast based on your measurements and observations. Check how accurate your forecast is.

Name: _____ Date: _____

STEAM Challenge Rubric

Directions: Think about the challenge. Score each item on a scale of 4 to 1. Circle your score.

4 = Always   3 = Often   2 = Sometimes   1 = Never

					Teacher Score
I used my materials appropriately. I chose materials I thought would work best.	4	3	2	1	
I was creative. I shared new ideas. I tried new ideas.	4	3	2	1	
I cooperated with others.	4	3	2	1	
I shared my thinking with others.	4	3	2	1	
I recorded my work, observations, and results.	4	3	2	1	
I followed directions.	4	3	2	1	
I persevered.	4	3	2	1	
I worked through the steps of the Engineering Design Process.	4	3	2	1	

Teacher Notes

_____

_____

_____

_____

Name: _____ Date: _____

Summative Assessment

Directions: Read the questions. Fill in or write the answers.

1. A group of engineers finish building a train. What should they do next?

- Ⓐ let people begin traveling on the train
- Ⓒ get feedback from other engineers
- Ⓑ test that it works safely
- Ⓓ build a second train

Explain your choice: _____

_____

2. You test an electromagnet you built to see if it will pick up staples. It does not work. What will you do next?

_____

_____

3. Which parts of the engineering design process do you think are most important? Choose two. Then, explain your choices.

- Ⓐ Research and Brainstorm
- Ⓓ Test and Evaluate
- Ⓔ Reflect
- Ⓑ Plan and Design
- Ⓕ Redesign
- Ⓒ Build and Create

_____

_____

Engineering Design Process

Understand the Challenge

Ask: What is the problem or need?

Research and Brainstorm

Learn more.
Think of different ideas.

Plan and Design

Make a sketch.
Label the parts and materials.

Build and Create

Gather materials.
Follow your plan.

Redesign

Plan and sketch a new design.

Test and Evaluate

Ask: Did it work? Did it meet the criteria?

Reflect

Ask: What went well? What can be better?

Share

Tell others about your design.

Digital Resources

Accessing the Digital Resources

The digital resources can be downloaded by following these steps:

1. Go to **www.tcmpub.com/digital**.

2. Use the ISBN number to redeem the digital resources.

   ISBN: 978-1-4258-2530-0

3. Respond to the question using the book.

4. Follow the prompts on the Content Cloud website to sign in or create a new account.

5. Choose the digital resources you would like to download. You can download all the files at once or a specific group of files.

Contents of the Digital Resources

- Safety Contract
- Sentence frames to help guide friendly student feedback
- Materials requests for students' families
- Student Glossary
- Materials list for the whole book

References Cited

Bybee, Rodger W. 2013. The Case for STEM Education: Challenges and Opportunities. Arlington, VA: NSTA Press.

NGSS Lead States. 2013. "Next Generation Science Standards: For States, By States APPENDIX I—Engineering Design in the NGSS." Washington, DC.